DATE DUE

Introduction to Local Area Computer Networks

K.C.E. Gee

The National Computing Centre Limited
Manchester

A WILEY-INTERSCIENCE PUBLICATION

JOHN WILEY & SONS
NEW YORK

First published 1983 by
The Macmillan Press Ltd
London and Basingstoke

Published in the USA by
Wiley-Interscience Division
John Wiley & Sons, Inc., New York

Printed in Great Britain

ISBN 0 471–80036–8

Contents

Acknowledgements

The National Computing Centre acknowledges with thanks the support provided by the Electronics and Avionics Requirements Board of the Department of Industry for the project from which this book derived.

1 *Introduction*

This book is about a particular class of techniques which can be used for connecting together computers and devices associated with computers. The computers can be any size ranging from a microprocessor incorporated into a typewriter, for example, up to the largest mainframe. Any device that needs to be used with a computer is relevant. The techniques are collectively known as local area networks (LANs) to distinguish them from other computer networks, since they are always confined to a limited geographic area, having typically a maximum cable length of a few kilometres. Another distinguishing characteristic of a LAN is that nowhere is use made of public services or facilities provided by national telecommunications authorities. The combinations of the limited distance and the freedom from constraints imposed by other authorities and organisations means that communications speeds many times greater than those found in typical national telecommunications circuits can be achieved.

This book is concerned with the techniques that can be employed to provide communications in this type of local environment. Although digital data transmission is currently the most important use seen for local area networks, some techniques can be extended to voice, text and visual information transmission, opening the door for integrating many forms of office communications within the one network.

Local area networks have been in limited use since the mid-1970s, but the drop in the price of electronic components and the increasing intelligence of the terminal devices used in computer systems have resulted in many more computer-based devices being installed in offices, schools, universities, factories, etc. The ability of computer-related devices to communicate with each other, access specialised services and devices, and share resources, increases their value enormously. Thus, users of relatively cheap intelligent devices based on microprocessors were soon looking round for an equally cheap method of interconnecting them. The local area networks then in existence appeared to be suitable, even though they had often been designed for other purposes, and soon they were being used for this new task with considerable success.

In size and appearance local area networks fall somewhere between the normal telecommunications networks and the hardware used to interconnect computer devices within the same room or cabinet. The techniques used for local area networks have been borrowed from both, but the end result is markedly different from either. However, several different solutions have been tried with the result that it is impossible at this stage to classify local networks as just another class of computer network. If that were true it would be possible to consider them within a book on the wider subject of computer communications. As it is, the number of different techniques and implementations in existence require that the subject be treated independently.

In this book it is assumed that the reader has some basic knowledge of computer communication techniques, although a detailed understanding is not necessary. Familiarity with normal computer use and an appreciation of the developments in terminals, work-stations and office equipment will also help to place local area networks into context.

Packet switching is one of the underlying principles of most modern local area networks and of many public data networks. A full treatment of packet switching is beyond the scope of this book, although its particular adaptation to local networking is discussed in some detail; similarly, the workings of the various access and transmission mechanisms are explained later in the book. The use of packet switching in the wider context, and in particular in public data networks, is best left to the specialist books on the subject; these are referred to at the appropriate place in the text.

Chapter 2 is concerned with filling in some of the background of computer networking and placing local area networks in their historical context. The following chapters go on to explain local networks by first examining the topologies that can be used (Chapter 3), basic data transmission techniques (Chapter 4), and the major requirements in terms of hardware and software (Chapter 5). Selected networks that have been implemented and extensively tested are described in Chapter 6. The remaining two chapters examine the expected and observed performance of local networks (Chapter 7) and their main application areas (Chapter 8).

Throughout the book the emphasis is on how local area networks work rather than on how they should be used. Because conditions of use and individual requirements vary so much, it is unlikely that any single networking technique will suit everyone, although in any particular environment it may appear to be ideal.

Local area networks have evolved very rapidly in a short time, but it is reasonably safe to assume that the techniques now in common use will remain since they have already undergone many years of development in research laboratories and elsewhere. The next development will be in the range of tasks to which local area networks can be applied and in the services that will be built in to the networks to help the end-user. This topic is discussed briefly at the end of the book.

2 *Characteristics of Local Computer Networks*

2.1 WHAT IS A LOCAL AREA NETWORK?

A local area network is distinguished from other networks by the area it serves, the speed at which information can be transmitted, the ease with which new devices can be added and the simplicity of the basic transmission medium itself.

A local area network can serve only a limited geographic area. Generally this is limited to a single building or a single works site. Typically the distances involved are of the order of a few hundred metres up to a kilometre or so.

Wide area networks can be built to carry data at a variety of speeds from a few hundred bits per second to several thousand, but local area networks are usually capable of transmitting information at several million bits per second.

A dream of many communications managers is to be able to connect up new devices without having to put in new cables each time and without having to implement new protocols and procedures on the host device. At this stage it is questionable whether the intelligence in the network will be sufficient to satisfy the latter requirements. Almost all current products in the area use a very simple form of cabling, frequently just a wire which runs around the building, sometimes with repeaters at intervals but often just as a plain wire.

This simple form of cabling is one of the most immediately obvious characteristics and possibly one of the most appealing. Potential buyers of local area networks should, however, be aware that simple cabling and simple connection procedures are only part of the story. To the end-user it is more important to have an efficient mechanism to transmit information without needing to know the technical details for interfacing to the network.

2.2 DEFINITIONS AND MAIN FEATURES

A local area network provides a data communications system that allows independent devices to communicate with each other. In this it is no different from other data networks. What distinguishes a local area network is that communication is confined to a limited area, wholly within one site in most instances. The site may be an office block, a floor of an office block, a factory, a university campus, etc. The number of devices served is limited and the whole network is under the control of a single organisation.

A local area network is best described by listing its major characteristics

- it is contained wholly within a limited geographic area,
- it interconnects otherwise independent devices,
- it provides a high degree of interconnection between the devices on the network,
- it is used for transmission of information, usually in digital form,
- inexpensive transmission media and devices are used to interface to the network,
- every device has the potential to communicate with every other device on the network.

Most, but not all, local area networks transmit information in a bit-serial form, rather than as parallel bit streams. The above description is not restricted to bit-serial networks.

Some features that have not been defined explicitly include

- the distances involved,
- the devices involved,
- the rate at which information is transmitted,
- the topology of the network,
- the physical medium used for transmitting the information,
- the protocols and access methods used,
- the existence or not of a controlling node.

Having said this we can fill in some of the details based on typical networks that are in existence, but since the topic is developing so rapidly it is conceivable that these may alter significantly as new techniques and uses are developed.

We have already discussed the devices that can be interconnected using local area networks, and the distances involved. We describe the remaining features in turn.

Transmission Rate

Data transmission rate 1–20 Mbps; although some systems are lower than this they are likely to be uprated soon.

Topologies

Two main topologies have emerged: bus and ring. Star-shaped networks are likely to become significant soon with the development of digital switched high-speed exchanges suitable for mixed data and voice traffic.

Transfer Media

The main transmission media currently in use are coaxial cable and twisted-pair telephone cable. There are practical problems to be overcome in the use of optical fibres before their use can become widespread.

Access Method

Two main access methods and network protocols are in use: (1) contention, carrier-sensing systems for use on shared bus networks, and (2) circulating empty slot systems for rings. Others are under development and will certainly appear in practical systems in the future. Especially relevant are the token-passing method (suitable for buses, rings and star topologies) and register insertion rings.

Controlling Nodes

At present few local area networks concentrate the control into a single controlling node, but with the rising importance of systems based on digital telephone exchanges the situation may change in the sense that the exchange will function as a central switch. It will not, however, perform the same functions as the network or communications controller in a typical computer network. These devices usually gave permission to use the network to all the other devices on it. The advanced digital exchange will act as a routeing and switching device, but possibly with extra facilities in the form of services available for all the other users.

2.3 SHORT HISTORY

Local area networks arose mainly in research and university environments. They form part of the continuing evolution of data transmission networks in general, and packet-switching technologies in particular.

Packet-switching techniques have attained a position of great importance during recent years following the early implementations in research systems, such as ARPA in the USA and at the National Physical Laboratory in the UK. Most national telecommunications authorities are now planning or have set up public networks that use packet-switching techniques, so the adoption of the ideas for local and private communication systems was to be expected.

Strangely, one of the first networks to be developed using the techniques that are now associated with local area networks was a very wide area network in which the cost and difficulty of providing normal cable links was prohibitively high. That system was the ALOHA network in Hawaii which was set up to provide cheap and easy access for a large number of terminal users to central computing facilities. The essential feature of the ALOHA system is the use of a broadcast radio channel by all the users. In the ALOHA network the terminal users contend with each other for use of the radio channel.

Packets of data are broadcast by the users and received by the central computer installation which is able to detect if two or more packets have collided by using the error check information in the packets. This scheme, known as Pure ALOHA, makes rather inefficient use of the available channel capacity resulting in, at best, a channel utilisation of less than 20 per cent.

A consideration of the poor channel utilisation gave rise to a development called the Slotted ALOHA system. In the Slotted ALOHA scheme the packet terminals are no longer allowed complete freedom to send packets. The time is divided up into segments and each terminal is allowed to start transmitting only at the beginning of the time segment. All the terminals on the system are synchronised with a master clock in the central computing site. The Slotted version results in a channel utilisation of around 40 per cent.

Following the early experience with the ALOHA network, other groups in the research area became interested in the different techniques for transporting data within a restricted geographic area. Notable among these was a group at the Palo Alto research laboratory of the Xerox Corporation in the USA. They took the basic idea used in the ALOHA network, that is, everybody shares the use of the same transmission medium, which they called the Ether. In their case the Ether is a network consisting of a single coaxial cable. The system they devised is now generally known as Ethernet and is discussed in much more detail in later sections.

Like ALOHA, Ethernet also uses a shared transmission medium but with different algorithms for accessing it and detecting and correcting collisions. Ethernet algorithms are claimed to ensure a much higher network utilisation. Figures in excess of 90 per cent have been observed under laboratory conditions.

Ethernet was not the only local area network under consideration in research establishments during the early 1970s. The Hasler company in Switzerland and the University of Cambridge Computing Laboratory in the UK were both experimenting with rather different approaches. In these all users on the network again share the same transmission medium, but instead of it being a bus configuration as in Ethernet, to which everybody has equal rights of access at any time, the Hasler and Cambridge systems were built around a loop of cable and the users could transmit only when they were given permission.

The latest developments in the field of local area networks are in the use of so-called broadband systems. A broadband network uses a technique of dividing the available bandwidth into separate channels, each of which is capable of carrying very high data transmission rates but without having to share with others. Its use as a local area network has been pioneered by the Mitre Corporation in the USA.

2.4 THE WIDER MARKET

While local area networks were being developed to meet particular requirements in specific research environments, the emphasis in computing changed during the 1970s from a single central high-powered mainframe computing system, which was available to all the users on that site and possibly elsewhere in the organisation, towards distribution of computing and the use of computer networks. The use of terminals proved a more convenient and cost-effective way of using computers than the earlier batch method, once the computer systems were capable of supporting several simultaneous users effectively. Early terminals contained the bare minimum of processing capability and were thus closely tied either to the computer itself or to a special-purpose terminal controller. The result was that computer networks were star-shaped, or made from several interconnected stars.

The development of powerful minicomputers with comprehensive operating systems and less stringent temperature and humidity requirements gave rise to the possibility of placing quite considerable computing power in several locations around an organisation, rather in concentrating it in one very small area.

There are a number of advantages in this approach

- reduced number of telecommunication circuits,
- special-purpose computers can be used which can suit the application better than a general-purpose mainframe,

- by limiting the amount of multiprocessing performed in any one machine the response at the terminals can be improved,
- the control and management of the device is in the hands of the end-user.

There are also disadvantages in distributed processing, some of the most important being

- managing the whole network and ensuring that standard techniques and equipment are used throughout, can be difficult,
- software development and modification is more difficult, especially where more than one make of machine is involved,
- high-level and low-level communications protocols are needed, information stored in one computer system is not immediately accessible to users of other systems.

However, many problems could be overcome by linking together the separate computers so that users on one system could still be able to use other systems. In this manner expensive resources, such as high-capacity disks or even special computers, could be shared by every user of the network. It was to meet just this situation that the Cambridge ring local area network was developed.

Distributed computing in this form soon became an accepted alternative to centralised mainframe computing, and manufacturers of computer systems, both minicomputers and mainframe systems, developed networking architecture to serve the needs. Each architecture was invariably built around one particular make of system, and often even around one particular range of devices. Networks with a mix of different computers and terminals are not served well by these products. The customers, on the other hand, saw the advantage of distributed computing networks in being able to use computers and their devices which had been obtained from a variety of sources, because in that way they could adapt the network to suit the applications.

When information on the experimental local area networks became known through conferences, etc., the users thought that possibly these could allow freer interconnection of equipment than had been possible before. Since local area networks are designed to use a standard network transport mechanism, it is certainly possible to move information from one device to another without bothering about different interfaces, device speeds, etc. But the information transported is still at best just a string of binary digits. Further levels of protocol are needed to make these strings understandable.

During recent years microprocessors have been developed at a very rapid rate and, at the same time, their price has fallen sharply. This has resulted in their being used for many purposes where it would have been uneconomic to use processors before. Many computer terminals now contain a range of sophisticated features made possible by the use of an internal microprocessor. Microprocessors are being used in more and more office equipment, ranging from fairly ordinary-looking typewriters to intelligent copiers and complex multipurpose workstations with personal-computing and information-handling facilities. Advantages can be realised similar to those mentioned earlier for distributed computing sytems if microprocessor-based devices can be linked together. A linked system provides many advantages for the individual devices, especially in the context of information storage and manipulation. Figure 2.1 shows a

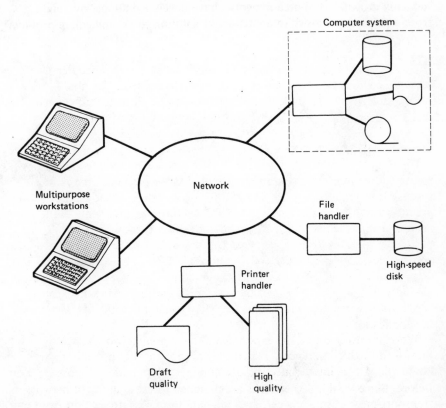

Figure 2.1 Office network

typical office system in which several multipurpose workstations all share a high-speed file-store with its associated file-manipulation routines. Also on the network are several special devices which are generally too expensive for use by individual workstations. The workstations themselves can be employed for word processing, file access, electronic mail, personal computing and accessing other computers and services. The file handler can also be used as a basis for an electronic mail system for the network.

The workstations in a typical office could be so numerous and inexpensive that a normal network constructed on the point-to-point dedicated line principle would be totally unsuitable. The number of lines needed would be too great to be installed economically, the transmission speed could well be too low, and the cost of each link would be a significant proportion of, or even exceed, the cost of the attached devices. Local area networks offer the almost ideal solution: cheap, easy to install, ubiquitous, extendable and providing complete device interconnection.

For this reason, more than any other, interest in local area networks has suddenly grown. Local area networks have developed almost overnight from a research curiosity to an attractive solution to an immediate problem.

3 *Network Topologies*

The topology of a network is the arrangement of the nodes and the inter-connections between them. A number of nodes can be interconnected in the following ways to form a network

Star   A central hub to which, or through which, all messages pass (figure 3.1a).

Ring   All the nodes are connected together in a ring, with none having overall control of access to the network (figure 3.1b).

Loop   All the nodes are connected together in a ring, but one of them controls the rest, and determines which should use the communications channel (figure 3.1c).

Bus (or highway)   A single communications circuit is shared by every node, but the circuit is not joined together to form a loop. Each node uses the bus to communicate with every other node (figure 3.1d).

Tree   The nodes are connected together by a branching communications channel. Again there are no loops on the network (figure 3.1d).

Mesh   When the nodes of the network are interconnected in a more complex manner which cannot easily be classified as one of the above, the network can be called a mesh. Some circuits may be shared for traffic between two pairs of nodes. For example, in figure 3.1e circuit X is used to carry traffic between A and B and between C and D.

Fully interconnected   When each node is directly connected to every other node in the network by a link that is not shared with any other (figure 3.1f), the network is said to be fully interconnected.

Various combinations of the above networks can be used, for example, several stars connected in a ring. But how important is the topology to an understanding of local area networks? We can consider this best by considering what local area networks are meant to achieve.

Local area networks typically exist to share resources; not only the resources available in the computing devices connected to it, but also the basic network transmission medium and sometimes a switching device. Of the network topologies mentioned above the star, ring and bus are those

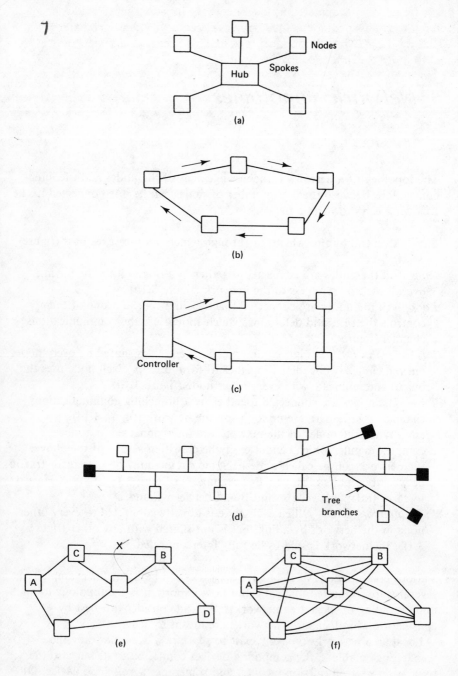

Figure 3.1 Basic topologies

most frequently encountered as local networks because they provide cheap interconnection of computers, computer-related devices and computer-based office products, while at the same time making it easy to add new devices and to move existing ones around.

Nodes that are in networks whose topologies are based on rings and buses share the transmission medium, that is, the circuit that connects all nodes together. Only one circuit is used and all messages passing between the nodes must go along it.

The star network approaches the problem by sharing the use of the central hub which either processes all the messages sent by the devices on the spokes of the star or acts as a routeing device to direct messages from one spoke to another.

The loop network, more commonly used for handling terminals using a large computer system, combines the sharing of a single unit controller and the interconnecting cable.

The other topologies cannot share a common communications resource among the users of the network, although they are often designed to share the resources of a computer system or an expensive peripheral device.

The main topologies found in local area networks will now be treated in more detail. Typical examples and details of the software and hardware needed to operate them are covered elsewhere in the book. Mesh and fully interconnected networks are generally not used for local area networks, so no further discussion of these will be included. The advantages and disadvantages of each topology are given in the descriptions. Two or more topologies, however, may share the same advantages.

3.1 STAR

A star-shaped network is illustrated in figure 3.1a. It is well known both as a typical computer network (figure 3.2), in which the centre of the star is a

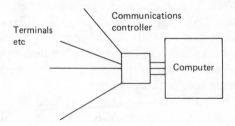

Figure 3.2 Star computer network

computer system that performs processing on information fed to it by the peripheral devices, and as a telephone system, in which the central hub is a switch that interconnects the different users on the network (figure 3.3).

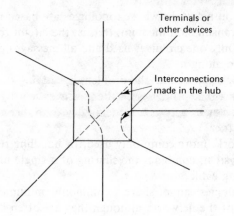

Figure 3.3 Switched hub star network

The first example illustrates the suitability of the star topology for the many-to-one approach, and the second its suitability for interconnecting pairs of devices. It is less suitable where several spokes require concurrent access to a device on another spoke.

If we take the broad view that local area networks exist to provide on-site communications between computer-based devices, then the star network is by far the most dominant class, since most existing computer systems have on-line access facilities to one or more central computers. However, local area networks are typically thought of as providing interconnection between all the devices on the network, something that is not always present in traditional computer-based networks. Such networks are typically operated by a device at the hub (which may be the computer itself or, more likely, a controller dedicated to handling terminals and peripheral devices); this controller asks, or polls, each device in turn to determine whether it has data to send. Only when the hub gives its permission can the devices on the spokes send the data. If the data are intended to go to another terminal, it is the usual practice in such systems for the computer at the hub to process the information and then send the message, rather than effectively just to switch the incoming line to that of the receiver so that messages can pass through without being processed by the hub.

The star-shaped network is also typical of the local telephone system that most offices and sites have already installed. The hub in this case is the private telephone exchange which nowadays is usually an automatic device (a PABX — Private Automatic Branch Exchange) that allows any telephone user to dial directly any other telephone. Frequently, facilities also exist for any user to dial an external line which can then be used to make telephone calls to any other number on the public telephone system. The PABX is a circuit-switching device because, based on the dialling information it receives from the telephone making a call, it connects together the caller's line to that of the one being called. Once the circuit is made it stays in existence until the conversation ends and the telephones are replaced, which indicates to the PABX to break the circuit. If a circuit joining two telephones already exists no other user can call either of those two telephones.

In the guise of the PABX, suitably enhanced, the star-shaped network is an important topology as a local area network. With the introduction of computer techniques and solid-state switching the PABX can be made to provide the kind of facilities required in a computer network. Fast switching allows circuits to be made and broken much more quickly than is possible with the older type of exchange so that it is feasible to set up a circuit just to transfer a line of text from a terminal to a computer. It need take only a fraction of a second to set up the connection, transfer the information, and break the circuit again. The link to the computer is then available for another terminal to use.

Although circuit switching is the traditional technique employed for the hub in the PABX-type of network it is possible for it to operate as a packet switching exchange.

A full description of packet switching is beyond the scope of this book. Readers who are interested in pursuing it further should consult one of the specialist books on the subject [1–3]. Here it will suffice to give a brief explanation of the advantages of packet switching and its application to the star topology.

Packet switching has in recent years been adopted as the normal method for transporting data over public data networks. Public data networks can be compared with public telephone networks since both are networks that serve a large community of users and provide a high-performance network at their heart shared by all the users. Public packet switched data networks (figure 3.4) use a number of exchanges situated at various places throughout the country, and all the users are connected to their nearest exchange. The exchanges themselves are interconnected by high-speed highly reliable circuits. Messages originating at a user site are broken down into conveniently sized blocks and put in a 'packet' that has the addresses of both the sender and the receiver. Packets are passed one by one to the packet switching exchange which sends them, interleaved with others from other users, to the exchange serving the destination device. On reaching the destination device they are checked for transmission errors, any packets containing errors are requested to be resent, and eventually the message is reassembled.

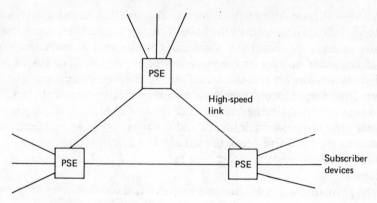

Figure 3.4 Packet switched network (PSE = packet switching exchange)

Although packet switching networks generally use more than one exchange, the concept can work just as well with a single exchange situated at the hub of a star network. Each device on the spokes can easily be in conversation with a number of different devices simultaneously, the interleaved packets travelling along the spoke being associated with different dialogues. This makes the technique especially suitable for stars that have one or more computer systems in the network.

The hub system at the centre of a star can perform functions other than normal data processing and line or message switching. For example, the hub can provide conversions of the data transmission speeds of the sender to that required by the receiver. The sender and destination devices may also operate using different communication protocols and character sets. The hub can act as a protocol converter, so allowing a terminal from one manufacturer to work successfully with a computer system from another.

One of the most significant aspects of a star network is the fact that much of the intelligence needed to control the network can reside in the one place and be shared by all the devices in the system. This enables dumb terminals to be used directly in the network, with each one operating at any speed it likes. No special logic is required to gain access to the circuits since each of the links is usually dedicated to the one device. It is conceivable, although not frequently encountered, that different media could be used for the links between the devices at the end of the spokes and the hub. For example, twisted-pair cable could be used for some links, coaxial and ribbon cables for others, and even optical fibres if the application demanded it.

The hub software could also provide a high degree of security protection to prevent unauthorised persons from using the network, or unauthorised terminals from accessing certain computer systems. If a link or end device develops a fault it is easy to identify which spoke contains the fault, report it to the network supervisor and disconnect it if necessary. Addressing is also simplified as each spoke corresponds to a particular device.

The facilities that the hub of an advanced star-shaped local area network could provide are ideal candidates for digital processing techniques applied to telephone exchanges. Developments are proceeding rapidly towards enhancing the traditional PABX functions and products on the market, sometimes called private computer or data exchanges, which incorporate some of the computing power mentioned above to handle data lines as well as providing the telephone switching functions of the ordinary PABX. The advantages of this approach are obvious: the data equipment can use the cables and ducts provided for the telephones, and the cost of the new PABX can often be justified on the telephone handling requirement alone, especially as it can enhance very significantly the telephone service in the office. As examples of the enhanced telephone functions provided, truncated numbers can be used to dial those subscribers who are most frequently called; the telephones can wait for a busy line to become free and then call the number; incoming calls can be automatically diverted to an alternative number if the normal telephone is not answered.

It must be recognised that the installation of a hub-controlled local area network may not always be the best solution. The hub itself, by virtue of the intelligence it requires to control even the simplest network, will be quite a costly item. If there is an adequate PABX already installed for the telephone services it could be difficult to justify its replacement with a PABX for both voice and data, or indeed the installation of another for data alone.

A star network is vulnerable to failures of the hub. For this reason most modern PABXs employ duplicates of the most essential components. Advocates of the PABX approach point to the high reliability required (and achieved) for normal PABXs and reason that the computerised ones must be as good if they hope to replace the existing ones. However unlikely the hub PABX is to fail, the possibility of such an occurrence is sufficient to deter many users who need to have a very reliable data-transmission network.

The cable network required by a star network is simple to visualise but generally difficult and costly to install when a large number of devices are being served. If the actual existing telephone cables can be used to handle data devices at an adequate speed without preventing the telephone from being used at the same time, then this problem is not serious. If new cables are required, then each device will need a separate line to the centre.

Summarising the features of the star-shaped local area network, the following are the main advantages and disadvantages.

Advantages

- ideal for many-to-one configurations,
- suited to dumb terminals,
- mixed transmission media and speeds can be used on the spokes,
- each spoke is independent of the rest,
- high security is possible,
- easy fault detection and isolation,
- addressing is easy, and is centrally controlled,
- cost can often be justified for voice alone,
- integration of data and voice (integration of office information handling).

Disadvantages

- vulnerable to central hub failures,
- complex technology required at the hub — hence expensive,
- ports are needed at the hub to handle all the lines — either on a one-to-
- one basis or shared,
- laying cables can be expensive,
- the newest technology must be used to obtain all the benefits,
- the data rates that can be handled are generally lower than ring or bus
- topologies, owing to the hub processing required.

Before leaving the description of the star local area network it is worth mentioning some of the other possibilities that have been suggested based on the central hub idea.

Illustrated in figure 3.5 is the so-called star-shaped ring. In this inter-connections between devices at any one time are by means of a ring, the

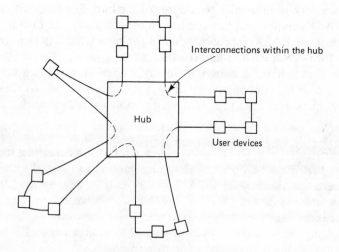

Figure 3.5 Star-shaped ring

features of which are discussed in a following section. But, every so often the ring passes through a central device that can be either unintelligent or intelligent. The unintelligent device merely provides the facility to detect and to isolate faulty sections of the ring, probably by manual means. If a small amount of intelligence is used then the control device could also perform as a ring monitor station. A well-designed hub with considerable intelligence could be made by including hardware and software to monitor continuously each of the segments and to switch out automatically those that are troublesome. The ring configuration and order in which data passes from device to device could also be changed very easily. The last feature also enables new devices to be aded to the ring without disturbing any users except those on the loop where the new device is being sited.

Further developments of the idea can be envisaged to allow the individual segments to be essentially separate rings (figure 3.6) with the hub device

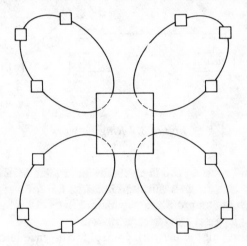

Figure 3.6 Rings connected as a star to a central hub

common to all. The individual rings could operate at different speeds, with the hub performing the conversions necessary when a device on one ring sends information to a device on another. Readers interested in these more exotic star-shaped rings should consult reference [4].

3.2 RING

A ring network is one in which each node is connected to two, and only two, other nodes. It is distinguished from the loop configuration by the fact that rings have no single node with overall authority over the others with regard to when they can send and receive messages, whereas a loop has a controlling node. Generally, rings do not join the end-devices themselves directly, for reasons that will be explained later. Instead, the ring consists of a series of repeaters or transceivers joined to each by the physical transmission medium, as shown in figure 3.7. End-user devices are connected to the repeaters.

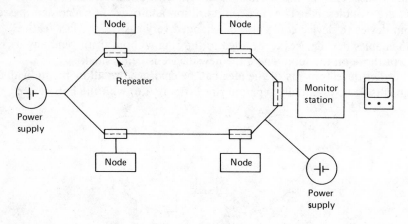

Figure 3.7 Ring network

The idea behind the ring topology for use in a local area network is to eliminate dependence on the central node at the hub of a star, while at the same time providing communications channels between all the devices on the network for high-speed data transmission.

Instead of putting all the network control intelligence into a single highly complicated and expensive switching node, each node on the network is associated with a repeater that can be made fairly simple with just sufficient logic to enable it to receive, transmit and make available to its node data or slots that are passing round the ring (figure 3.8). Messages, or blocks of information, once placed on the ring, are continuously regenerated as they pass through each repeater and will circulate for ever unless removed or flagged as available for other nodes. Usually, the original sender of the information is made responsible for its removal.

There are many ways of operating a ring but at the superficial level they are reasonably similar, at least to the end-user. The different mechanisms for accessing and controlling the ring are discussed in detail in Chapter 5. For the time being we shall concentrate on the common features and how these differ from those used for other local area network topologies.

Rings almost always transmit in one direction only all the time. There is no absolute necessity for this but in practice it makes the design of the

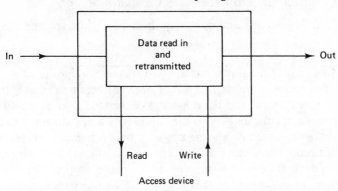

Figure 3.8 Schematic view of a ring repeater

repeaters much easier, and it requires much less sophisticated data transmission protocols to ensure that the information reaches its destination correctly and in sequence with other parts of the same message. The repeaters themselves are usually made so that they can transmit and receive simultaneously, thus preventing transmission delays and ensuring that full-duplex working is possible.

Unlike some other local area network topologies, routeing between nodes is trivial since there is generally only one path in to and out from a repeater. All messages must go by that route. Messages and the permission to use the ring to transmit pass sequentially around the ring from one node to the next. This happens regardless of the bandwidth available and it ensures that each node has a fair share of the available network capacity.

Broadcasting messages to all locations on the ring is simple since every node is capable of receiving every message put on the ring. It is an easy task to arrange for a special address to be used to designate broadcast messages. However, unless explicit acknowledgements are sent by all the nodes, the sender has no way of knowing which nodes were switched on and so which did in fact receive the message.

The cost of installing a ring is one of the lowest for local area networks. Normal telephone grade twisted-pair cable is often used and the repeaters can be made relatively simple. One of the best known examples of a local ring is that designed and installed at the University of Cambridge Computer Laboratory. This ring uses two pairs of twisted-pair cable, a simple-to-implement transmission technique, together with simple repeaters.

Using two pairs of cable enables a simple signalling method to be used and power can be carried to the repeaters. Cambridge ring repeaters should not be more than 100 metres apart in order to minimise phasing problems caused by dissimilarities in length and other factors between the pairs of cable. By carefully selecting and matching the cables wider spacing can be achieved.

Because rings usually transmit in only one direction they are ideal for the application of optical fibre links, but the cost of these is significantly greater than for ordinary wires. The use of optical fibres necessitates the use of optical-to-electrical (and the opposite) converters, optical amplifiers, and so on; these add considerably to the complexity and reduce the overall reliability. The repeaters must also be powered by a separate cable since optical fibres cannot carry any power. Tapping a new node into the optical fibre is not so straightforward as tapping a wire cable. Optical fibres are especially useful in environments that are electrically noisy because they are immune to electromagnetic radiation. The Cambridge ring at the Computer Laboratory has a section of optical fibre, which illustrates that the transmission medium of a ring can be made up of sections of different materials without causing undue problems.

Doubts about reliability are the main criticisms usually levelled at the ring topology. The operation of the network relies on the working of every single link and repeater. It is possible to construct rings that use extra paths to bridge sections of the ring that are liable to fail, either through a broken link or a failed repeater. One method is illustrated in figure 3.9, where each

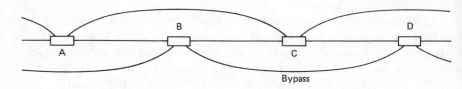

Figure 3.9 A way to bypass failed links and repeaters

repeater is bypassed by a link which joins the repeaters on either side of it. If repeater C fails, or links B–C or C–D break, then the bypass circuit shown will be switched in either manually or automatically. The limitations of this technique are that if two or more sections fail side by side the bypass will not work unless another longer-hop bypass section is used, and the length of the bypass cannot exceed the maximum allowed spacing of the repeaters.

Although it is not necessary from a design point of view, a monitor node has been found to be essential in practice in most types of ring. The monitor generally exists primarily to remove packets that have been damaged in such a way that the sender cannot recognise them, or to remove packets that were sent out by a node that has since ceased operation. The monitor will also start up the ring, send round testing packets, and monitor error packets received from other nodes. Some of the ring techniques require other housekeeping tasks that can similarly best be performed by the monitor.

When new nodes are added to an existing ring its operation is temporarily interrupted. The interruption may be minimised by building jack sockets into the ring so that repeaters can simply be plugged in without the ring ceasing operation first. The plugging in will usually cause a brief discontinuity in transmission but the normal error handling procedures built into the methods of use are sufficient to keep the ring operating without users noticing the interruption. If no jack sockets exist the ring has to be broken, as it is not possible to put a passive tap into it.

Lengthening the ring can be awkward, although the transmission techniques used do not normally limit the maximum allowed length. The problems arise in the physical installation of a new section of cable which must be routed in such a way that the ring topology is preserved. For this reason, offices and sites that use ring topologies usually try to install them initially so that every conceivable point where the ring is likely to be used is reached. Compared with the bus topology, the cabling and its installation are more complex, but this is largely offset by the much simpler repeaters or transceivers that are needed.

To summarise, the advantages and disadvantages of the ring topology are given below.

Advantages

- the transmission capacity is shared fairly among all the users,
- there is no dependence on a central device,
- error-generating links and nodes can be easily identified,
- routeing is trivially simple,
- checking for transmission errors is easy,
- automatic confirmation of receipt is easy to implement,
- broadcasting to all nodes is easy,
- access is guaranteed, even when the ring is heavily loaded,
- error rate is very low,
- very high transmission rates are possible,
- mixed transmission media can be used.

Disadvantages

- reliability depends on the whole loop and the repeaters,
- a monitoring device is usually needed in practice,
- it is difficult to add new nodes without disrupting the operation of the ring,
- it is difficult to lengthen the ring,
- repeaters must impose some signal delay,
- repeaters must normally be quite close together,
- cable installation and routeing can be complex.

In conclusion, let us remember that the appeal of the ring topology was originally to provide a cheap and easy-to-operate means of interconnecting both intelligent and dumb devices within the confines of a single site. It should be impossible for any one device to get an unfair share of the available capacity. The data transmission rate should also be more typical of the speeds at which computers operate rather than normal telecommunication speeds. Most ring technologies that have been developed achieve these goals at reasonable cost.

3.3 LOOP

A loop is very similar to the ring in concept and actual shape, but the difference lies in the method by which the nodes are able to use the shared transmission medium. A loop is shown in figure 3.10. One node is given

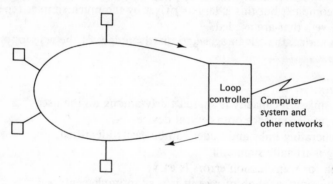

Figure 3.10 Loop network

overall control in deciding which node can use the circuits and for what purposes. This can be achieved by sending polls out to each node in turn or by various other techniques, such as sending out an empty packet that is available for any device to use.

Loops are best suited to handling low-speed devices such as terminals. In these the controller will be responsible for a number of terminals that will probably be connected to a remote computer system. The controlling device will be part of another network, possibly a star with the main computer system at the centre and the loop controllers at the end of the spokes.

Since the control is concentrated in one place, the relative priorities of the devices on the loop can be set and controlled very easily. The use of repeaters on loops is rare since the access is centrally controlled, the loops are usually short, and the transmission speeds are low.

Because the transmission medium is shared by all the devices, a loop can be thought of as a local area network, but loops have been in use for some considerable time, long before local area networks became fashionable. Loops have their origins in on-line access to mainframe or minicomputer systems since they are a development of the polled multipoint line principle. For this reason, and because of the active part taken by the controller in controlling access to the network, the transmission speed is generally much lower than those found in most other local area network topologies. Since loops usually serve low-speed terminals this is not a problem, and it is very rare to see a loop used to link several intelligent devices requiring a high data-transmission speed. For them the ring or bus techniques have more appeal. There is no real reason why loops should not employ high-speed links, in which case many more devices per loop could be handled, provided that suitable methods could be devised to share the capacity fairly without losing too much time in polling all the devices, most of which will have no data to send most of the time.

Advantages

• very suitable for connecting devices with limited intelligence,
• low cabling costs,
• well-known mainframe terminal handling procedures are used,
• it is simple to add new devices.

Disadvantages

• system depends on the controller for its operation,
• low data-transmission speeds,
• communications are generally device ↔ controller, and not directly
• device ↔ device.

3.4 BUS

The basic form of the data bus or highway is shown in figure 3.11. It consists of a single section of cable that has two discrete ends to it — that

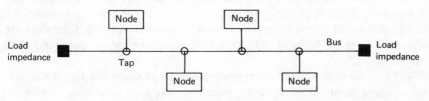

Figure 3.11 Bus or highway network

is they are not joined together to form a loop. Devices are attached to the bus at intervals. Although the word 'node' may appear to be inappropriate for a bus since these points do not necessarily lie at the junctions of the cable, it can be used to indicate the positions at which the cable is tapped and where one or more devices are attached through the necessary interface units. 'Station' is a more appropriate word, but in this section station and node will be used interchangeably. Information is transmitted to the bus by a node and the signals propagate to all parts of it at about three-quarters of the speed of light. All nodes attached to the bus can hear every transmission being made. In this manner the bus is similar to normal radio broadcast transmissions in which one or a number of transmitters have access to the airwaves through their aerials. Their transmission can be heard by any receiver built to receive them.

The other way of using a bus is familiar to all users of domestic radio and television receivers. In these the airwaves are shared by a number of simultaneous transmissions that use different frequency bands, so that they can readily be distinguished by receivers tuned to the appropriate frequency. Provided that the frequencies used are not too close together, there is little or no interference experienced between channels. Bus networks that use the same principle with a cable substituted for the airwaves are sometimes called *broadband* bus networks.

The different implications of the two methods are so significant that it is worthwhile considering baseband and broadband bus networks separately.

3.4.1 Baseband Bus

Baseband means that the signal is unmodulated and so digital information is broadcast as a series of pulses that represent zeros and ones. The technique is explained in Chapter 4.

Baseband in the local area network context means that the networks do not use frequency division multiplexing of the bandwidth but instead divide up the time interval in some manner between all the users. At any given time only one node can transmit to the bus. If two or more try to use it at the same instant the information from each one of them is damaged and must be retransmitted. Thus time division multiplexing is the technique that is adopted, but the responsibility for allocating the time slots is usually distributed to all the nodes on the network. The ways in which the slots are allocated form the basis of the different techniques used for baseband bus transmission.

The bus medium is itself completely passive and there is no need for any active components in the medium, such as converters, repeaters, amplifiers or modulators. The medium, if it is a cable, is usually terminated at both ends by electrical loads of the correct type in order to prevent spurious reflections that would interfere with the transmission and prevent the signal from dying away quickly.

For the larger networks, and when separate networks need to be interconnected, some special amplifiers and repeaters may be needed, but they can affect the normal characteristics of the network so much that they require special consideration depending on the transmission technology and access technique used.

Figure 3.12 shows a typical method of connecting to a baseband bus. The cable tap is there to make an electrical or electromagnetic connection to the

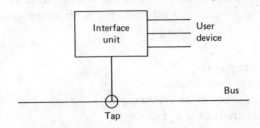

Figure 3.12 Attaching to a bus

transmission medium. It is equivalent to a radio aerial in the analogy with radio transmission. Since the usual transmission medium for baseband systems is coaxial cable it is possible to make the tap so that it does not actually break the wire. This is advisable since breaks can alter the electrical characteristics significantly, causing serious effects on a network carrying many millions of bits per second. The interface unit shown in figure 3.12 performs the task of converting the data stream from the form needed by the attached device to that required for transmission over the network. It puts the data from the attached device into the correct packet format, together with the appropriate source and destination addresses, error-checking and other control information; it then transmits it to the medium at the right time, retransmitting it if it collides with another packet and the access method used demands it. The interfaces are discussed in more detail in Chapter 5.

What is significant about the way in which the nodes interface to a baseband bus is that all the access and interfacing hardware and software are external to the transmission medium, so nodes can be attached practically anywhere on the network without affecting any of the others. The cable taps are made so that they introduce the minimum of electrical disturbance to the other devices when they are being attached. In practice the presence of each new tap does alter the transmission characteristics slightly; systems therefore impose restrictions on the number of taps allowed and where they can be made.

All devices on a baseband bus hear all the transmissions on the network. The interface unit has the job of extracting those that are addressed to the device it serves while ignoring the rest. Messages can easily be broadcast to every node; all it requires is a special address or flag to be placed in the control information fields of the packet which every node can recognise.

Bus access control can be centralised by polling or switching, but it is much more common for it to be distributed. In the University of Hawaii ALOHA system the messages were, naturally, all broadcast, but the central system in Honolulu contained a message switch so that one device did not send messages directly to another but always used the central system.

Despite all the problems the baseband bus is a network with a lot of appeal, as a consideration of its advantages and disadvantages will show.

Advantages
- medium is totally passive,
- it is easy to attach new devices,
- good use can be made of available capacity, 2
- the components are readily available,
- installation is easy — no complex routeing problems, tap on
- system is suited to traffic in bursts,
- several low-speed devices can be interfaced through a single interface unit.

Disadvantages
- anyone with the right equipment can listen to the medium without being detected or disrupting the normal operation, 1
- intelligence is needed to interface to the medium, 2
- ordinary terminals can only be connected through sophisticated interface units,
- messages sometimes interfere with each other, 3
- no automatic acknowledgement of receipt,
- there is no fairness built in to the system since, unless it is centrally controlled, the nodes can use the medium whenever it is free,
- the total length of the bus is limited, usually to around 1 or 2 km, but
- this depends on so many factors that it is dangerous to generalise.

3.4.2 Broadband Bus

As explained earlier a broadband bus is rather like the radio airwaves in which different frequencies are allocated to different services. In the bus network the airwaves are replaced by a cable (almost always coaxial) which carries radio-frequency (RF) transmissions of data suitably modulated on to carrier waves. The transmitters and receivers that are used for normal radio transmission are replaced by RF modems in a broadband bus network.

The techniques of using the broadband bus are explained in chapter 4 when discussing transmission techniques.

The broadband technology has been used for many years in the cable television industry, called CATV (Community Antenna TeleVision) in the USA. In this a single length of coaxial cable is used to carry several television channels simultaneously to many subscribers from a single receiver with an aerial. The cable network can cover a wide area, since RF analogue transmission is used which can be amplified whenever the signal strength falls too low. The cable need not be a single unbranched length but can branch as much as necessary, provided that it does not form any closed loops. In CATV each channel is allocated a single-frequency band (6–8 MHz is needed to carry real-time colour television pictures).

The techniques of using the broadband bus are explained in Chapter 4 can cover a very wide area, equipment is easy to obtain and is extremely rugged and reliable, and the cable bandwidth can be split to allow it to carry data, video, voice, and so on — both analogue and digital.

Advantages
- medium and interface devices are easy to obtain, 4
- long distances can be covered,
- it is easy to extend, add new branches, and add new devices,
- suited to continuous high-speed traffic, 3
- suited, by means of contention techniques, to other kinds of data traffic,
- can mix video, data, voice, and so on — all on the one cable,
- easy to install and route the cable, 1
- headend can be made intelligent.

Disadvantages
- modems are costly,
- most practical implementations need a headend operating continuously,
- line amplifiers or repeaters need to be powered reliably.

3.5 TREE

The tree topology is essentially a series of buses connected together. Usually there is a central backbone bus to which a number of smaller branch buses are connected, as shown in figure 3.13. The backbone is tapped by suitable splitters and the nodes and end devices are attached to the network by the same methods employed for standard bus systems.

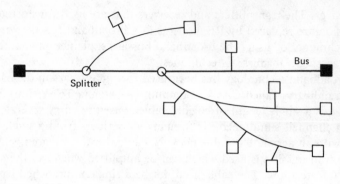

Figure 3.13 Tree network

In its basic form just described, the tree network is best suited to the broadband method since the transmissions are modulated analogue signals — two frequency channels being used, one for transmitting and the other for receiving. Cable splitters and signal amplifiers are easily fitted to a broadband bus, with few problems being caused by signal reflections and loss of power owing to the extra devices.

Baseband buses are much more difficult to handle when extra devices, even as simple as cable connectors, are inserted in the cable run. A branch will mean that the signal will be propagated in two different parts which, unless they are perfectly matched, will travel at different speeds and will be reflected in different ways. Baseband systems that allow tree structures are generally run at much lower speeds than those with a single bus; they also usually use a different type of cable. Single bus systems generally use coaxial cable with matched load impedances at the ends. Multicore cable is often employed in systems that permit a tree topology; here one wire is used to indicate to the others that the network is being used by one of the nodes. The others are used to carry separately the data and timing signals.

Another technique adopted for baseband buses is to insert repeaters, but limit the number allowed between any two nodes. The technique adopted by Ethernet, the most advanced baseband project, is shown in figure 3.14. One bus is designated as the backbone. Devices can be attached to this in the normal way, but signal repeaters are also attached, and through them signals pass to the branch buses. No further connections to repeaters from the branches are allowed. Thus, the greatest number of repeaters that a signal must pass through between any two nodes is two. The backbone bus would, for example, run through a lift shaft or service duct accessible from every floor of any office block. Each floor has its own bus which is attached through a repeater to the backbone bus.

Apart from these restrictions the tree topology has the same advantages and disadvantages as a standard bus.

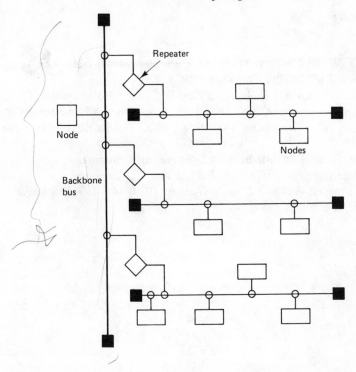

Figure 3.14 Practical implementation of tree-shaped baseband bus (Ethernet)

3.6 CONCLUSIONS

Local area networks are usually stars, rings, bus or tree networks because these offer the best compromise between cost, resilience and efficiency. Fully interconnected and mesh networks require too much cabling and are too complex to install and control for them to be commonly adopted in this context. There are circumstances, however, where the application demands a highly resilient and organised network to support it. These are beyond the scope of this book.

Any network requires far more than a few cables to make it perform as the end-user wants. In the next chapter we shall discuss some of the more common transmission techniques used, and how these have been applied to local area networks.

REFERENCES

1 Davies, D. W. and Barber, D. L. A., *Communications Networks for Computers*, John Wiley, Chichester, 1973.
2 Davies, D. W., Barber, D. L. A., Price, W. L. and Solomonides, C. M., *Computer Networks and their Protocols*, John Wiley, Chichester, 1979.
3 Bleazard, G. B., *Why Packet Switching?*, NCC Publications, Manchester, 1979.
4 Penney, B. K. and Baghdadi, A. A., 'Survey of Computer Communication Loop Networks: Parts 1 and 2', *Computer Communications*, Volume 2 No. 4 (August 1979) 165–180; Volume 2 No. 5 (October 1979) 224–241.

4 *Data-transmission Technologies*

It is only comparatively recently that telecommunications have become widely used with computers. Before that data to be processed by computer were laboriously put into a form that the computer could read and understand. Punched cards or paper tape were usually employed, although to meet special requirements magnetic tape disks were sometimes used. Output came as printed paper, punched cards or tapes, or on magnetic media. Paper output, the most common form, was collected from the personnel who tended the computer. Information was read from the output and often copied out on to punching instructions ready for input to another program. Jobs were collected together in batches and read into the computer for processing at some later time. Under this system turnaround was slow, especially when a missing or misplaced input card meant that the whole job failed and had to be rescheduled.

The only data communications used by early computer systems were between parts of the same system (for example, between the central processor and the input/output controllers). The distances involved were very short but the data-transfer rate needed to be very high; therefore special techniques were employed which were not suitable for use on normal telecommunication circuits.

It was some time before users and designers placed input and output devices a long distance away from the computer itself. The standard telecommunications circuits available to them appeared to be wholly unsuited to the needs of computer systems since they were designed for low-quality speech transmission in an analogue waveform. Modern computers are always digital, so the problems of taking a high-speed digital data stream and converting it into a form suitable for transmision over circuits designed for analogue signals had first to be overcome.

In this chapter we shall examine the basic problems of data transmission over medium and long distances and how these have successfully been overcome. The techniques used for short-distance communications within computer systems lie outside the scope of this book, although some of the ideas have been taken up by designers of local networks. These will be discussed in section 4.2 where we shall examine in detail the techniques that have been applied to and developed for local area networks. The chapter will end with a brief examination of the physical media that have been used for local communications.

4.1 BASIC TECHNIQUES

Data transmission is a very large subject, local area networks being but one small aspect. The basic principles are presented in this section in a very abbreviated form, but good introductions to the subject are available [1, 2]. Further descriptions of data transmissions, in the particular context of public services, including the use of the telephone system, can be found in reference [3]. This and the following sections will concentrate on those aspects of data communications that have a direct bearing on the systems used for local area networks.

Data transmission requires the designer to do much more than simply link computers and terminals to opposite ends of a wire or telephone circuit. To understand the problem it is necessary to examine the characteristics of the normal telecommunications facilities.

The normal telephone network forms the basis of many telecommunications systems used for computers for the very good reason that it already existed and was readily available when experiments were first started on data transmission. The Telex network appeared to be more suitable but the rate at which data could be transported made it unsuitable for most applications. The telephone network was built to serve a totally different set of requirements from those imposed by computers. The most obvious difference is the form of the signals produced by telephones and by computers. A voice signal has an analogue waveform which is transmitted by electrical circuits using varying voltages on the line (see figure 4.1). For

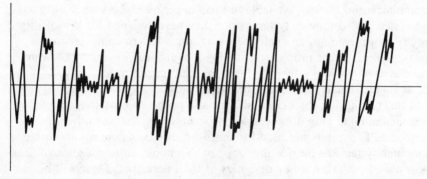

Figure 4.1 Speech signal

various reasons only a limited range of frequencies can be transmitted, typically 300–3400 Hz for the national telephone system. The bandwidth of an ordinary circuit is the difference between the highest and lowest frequency that can be handled — in this case it is 3100 Hz. Although this may seem to be narrow when compared with the range of sounds that a human ear can hear (200–20000 Hz), most of the information content of speech is contained in the 300–3400 band. The sound carried by the telephone network is usually understandable and even the voice of the user is recognisable.

Transmission media all have a bandwidth that is limited to a greater or lesser extent, but not only does the medium itself limit the bandwidth it also limits the devices that are attached to it. This limited bandwidth has important repercussions on the transmission of digital data, as will be seen later.

A square wave (figure 4.2a) is composed of an infinite number of sine waves made up from the basic frequency of the wave (n Hz say) on to which all the odd harmonics $3n$, $5n$, $7n$, ... are superimposed with decreasing amplitude. Transmitting such a wave on a medium with a restricted bandwidth will result in distortion mainly owing to the higher-frequency components being attenuated and delayed more than the lower ones. The result is shown in figure 4.2b.

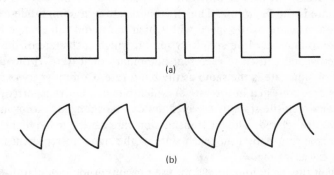

(a)

(b)

Figure 4.2 The effects of limited bandwidth on the transmission of a square wave: (a) input, (b) output

Computer-generated information is digital in form, although not periodic like a true square wave. However, when transmitted, it has much of the character of a square wave. It follows that the problems of transmitting it in a recognisable form are similar to those associated with the transmission of periodic square waves. Distortion of the information can be so severe that the actual distinction between a zero and a one can easily be lost unless special techniques are employed to overcome the problems.

Since transmission circuits are inherently unsuitable for transmitting digital information, why not convert the digital information into an equivalent analogue waveform that lies within the permissible bandwidth before transmitting it? This is the underlying principle of data transmission using telecommunications circuits and is the technique employed by the *modem*. The word modem stands for *mod*ulator/*dem*odulator, which describes its function. Digital information is converted into a series of different analogue signals (the modem modulates it) for onward transmission. The analogue signals are converted back into their digital equivalent (demodulated) at the destination. Many methods of modulating digital signals are used.

Amplitude modulation   The amplitude of a fixed frequency carrier wave is altered to match the incoming bit pattern.

Frequency modulation   The frequency of the carrier wave is varied either side of a mean value to represent the bits.

Phase modulation   In this technique the phase of the carrier wave is altered when the bits change from one value to another.

It is obvious that the modems used to terminate a circuit must both use the same modulation technique and operate at the same speed.

A measure of the rate at which the medium and driving devices can change state is the *baud rate*. Thus the baud rate in an amplitude-modulated system is a measure of the speed with which the signal can change from one amplitude to another. In a simple system in which each state of the modulated signal is used to represent one binary digit (0 to 1) the maximum bit transmission rate is the same as the baud rate. Computer users and designers are interested in the rate at which bits can be transported, not in the rate at which the state of the medium can be changed, except in so far as the two are related. The bit transmission rate can be made higher than the baud rate simply by using each state of the signal to represent more than one bit at a time.

Although this technique is seldom used in amplitude modulation systems, figure 4.3 shows how four amplitudes can be used to represent four pairs of values: 00, 01, 10 and 11. It is possible to use more than four states to carry progressively more information, but the more states that are used, the more sophisticated must be the modems to detect the differences in state among all the noise and random signals produced in the transmission network. For these reasons, frequency and phase modulation techniques are preferred for the higher transmission rates.

Modems are complex devices and details of the way that they are used in analogue networks such as the public telephone network and on leased circuits are best left to the specialised books on the subject. Readers interested in pursuing the subject further are recommended to read references [3] and [4].

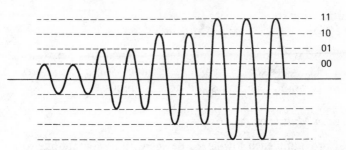

Figure 4.3 Amplitude modulation with four levels

For the purpose of this book special data-transmission techniques need to be considered. Typically, digital data devices (terminals, computers, etc.) produce information in bursts for short periods. However, during these bursts data is output at high speed. The data-transmission circuits must be capable of handling transmissions at the highest rate that will be presented to them, rather than at the average rate, over a long period of time. Naturally, modems and circuits suitable for the higher transmission rates are much more expensive than those suitable for low rates. To overcome the cost problem several devices may share the use of one high-speed circuit by means of intermediate devices called multiplexers and concentrators.

The difference between a multiplexer and a concentrator used to be quite clear, but as techniques have developed and more intelligence has been introduced into these devices so the distinction has become blurred. It has now become commonplace to use the terms interchangeably. Before this happened, however, *multiplexing* was used to refer to schemes in which time slots or frequency bands on a channel being shared were assigned on a fixed and predetermined basis. *Concentration* was used for systems in which a number of devices share a common set of output channels on a demand basis. The concentrator had to incorporate a certain degree of intelligence and buffering to allow it to allocate output channel capacity without significantly affecting the input devices. A simple multiplexer makes rather inefficient use of the capacity of the output channel unless all its attached devices are sending data all of the time. A concentrator can enable devices to make better use of the capacity of the channel. Multiplexing techniques have been developed to improve the efficiency of the line utilisation by employing intelligent multiplexers which perform functions similar to concentrators. Hence the use of the words multiplexing and concentration interchangeably.

4.1.1 Multiplexing

Multiplexing is of fundamental importance to local area networks since the network resources are shared by a large number of individual users. Some of the more common techniques will now be discussed.

Time-division Multiplexing

Instead of providing each low-speed device with a separate line to a computer or other system, a straightforward time-division multiplexer is often employed. The multiplexer allocates to each of the attached devices a unique time slot during which it has exclusive use of the high-speed circuit that is shared by all. The devices generate data at their own rate and so the time slots are made fairly small in order that each one can use the shared circuit frequently. The quantity of buffer storage required in the multiplexer can be minimised by this technique. Another multiplexer is required at the other end of the circuit to unscramble the data stream and reassemble the outputs of each of the individual devices.

Time-division multiplexing in this simple form is found on local area networks, especially those based on ring-shaped topologies. In these each station on the ring is normally given the opportunity to use the ring for a fixed time interval. The multiplexing function is not performed by a physically separate device but is inherent in the mechanism used for accessing the ring.

Statistical Time-division Multiplexing

Time-division multiplexing in which fixed time slots are used can be inefficient unless every device being multiplexed is transmitting or receiving all the time. This is extremely unlikely to occur in practice. The principle behind statistical time-division multiplexing is that time is only allocated to devices when they actually require it. The devices connected to a statistical time-division multiplexer actually contend with each other for use of the shared link. The multiplexer must obviously contain sufficient intelligence to be able to determine which device is requesting time, and to perform the usual multiplexing function of allocating time slots when more than one device wants to use the circuit at the same time. It is statistically very unlikely that all the devices will be wanting to use the shared circuit at the same time, so a circuit of a given capacity can support more devices than would be possible using a fixed time-division multiplexing system.

This assumption that it is extremely unlikely that every device on a network will want to transmit at the same instant underlies many of the local area network sharing mechanisms. In particular local area networks that use the carrier-sensing multiple access methods use essentially statistical time-division multiplexing. The time slots on the network are determined by the length of the packet being transmitted and are allocated on demand from the devices wishing to transmit. The intelligence that is needed to allocate the channel to the individual devices is contained in the interface units associated with each attached device, and does not reside in a single autonomous multiplexer.

Frequency-division Multiplexing

It was mentioned earlier that every channel used for transmission has a certain frequency bandwidth, which is extremely small on the telephone network, but adequate for its designed mode of use. Some circuits can have very wide bandwidths, of the order of several hundred MHz for coaxial cable. With a wide bandwidth it is possible to divide the band up into several smaller bands each with sufficient bandwidth to be adequate for the digital data transmission rate chosen for it. Between each frequency band, narrower bands are required to minimise interference between adjacent bands.

Using frequency-division multiplexing a number of individual channels with low bandwidth requirements can share the wide bandwidth provided by some transmission media. The technique has been applied to the so-called broadband-type of local area network in which one or two coaxial cables with 300–400 MHz usable bandwidth are employed. Various ways of using the individual channels have been devised, ranging from allocating set channels to a predetermined pair of users, to channels which are shared using time-division multiplexing techniques by a group of relatively slow-speed devices. Frequency-division multiplexing applied to local area networks also allows for analogue transmissions (for example, voice and television) to share the same network without first having to be digitised.

The details of broadband local area networks and their use of frequency-division multiplexing will be presented in section 4.2.2 and Chapter 6.

4.1.2 Data Link Protocols

So far only the physical characteristics of the transmission media have been discussed, but once it has been decided how to link two devices, and how to share the circuit with others, some techniques must be devised to ensure that the digital information is transmitted at the correct time, in the right order, and in such a manner that transmission errors can be detected and corrected. These are the essential ingredients of *data link protocols*.

On a point-to-point link that is not shared with other users the information stream can be output with just sufficient control information to permit the sender and receiver to keep in step and understand what actions to take. For example, get ready to receive, end the message, jump to the beginning of a new line, etc. The data link protocols needed for this type of circuit can be very simple and still perform adequately. In the discussions on multiplexing the various techniques in common use require that the information stream for transmission over a shared channel be split up into small blocks before being placed on the network. This technique is often called *framing* and is particularly relevant to local area networks.

To place modern data-framing techniques in context the simpler character-based message protocols will be described first.

Early computer terminals contained little or no intelligence and each character keyed in by the user was represented by a group of binary digits which was then transmitted. To help the equipment at the other end of the circuit to recognise the start and end of the character, special bit sequences were used to mark them. The start and stop sequences were typically two bits each in length. This technique was not very suitable for situations in which several characters needed to be transmitted in sequence close together. To meet this latter requirement *synchronous* techniques are used in which the sender and receiver agree to send characters at a known rate, so eliminating the need for start and stop delimiters for each one. The characters are assembled into blocks and the whole block delimited before transmission. In order to keep the sender and receiver in step the whole time, they need to send synchronisation characters continuously whenever there is no true data to transmit. In practice most implementations of character protocols also put in a synchronisation character every so often into the data stream in order to reset the internal clock of the receiver.

As well as the characters used to convey information (mainly alphabetic and numeric) some special characters are required to control the devices involved. The most obvious examples are the characters used to position the print carriage and print head. The devices involved have to scan continuously the input for control characters.

Character-based protocols are suited to slow-speed relatively unintelligent devices that produce the normal range of keyboard characters. For more complex situations, involving computers communicating with other computers or controllers for example, more complex protocols are required.

Various extensions of the character-based protocols have been made to suit various purposes. The protocol known as *basic mode* is the basis of the most advanced of these techniques. In basic mode the characters are put into blocks, a header is placed at the front and a trailer at the end. The header can be used to hold an address so that several devices can share a single circuit and each one can be polled individually by a controlling device. The basic mode protocol contains more than just a definition of the way the messages are framed. It also contains definitions of the rules which each device must follow in order that an orderly exchange of information can take place.

None of the above procedures is particularly relevant to local area networks found today. However, they illustrate the state of protocol development when it was decided that the restrictions imposed by character-based procedures were constraining further developments of data-transmission networks.

In 1968 a new technique for data-transmission protocols was proposed, based on the use of a single frame structure which would be used to convey data and control information in separate fields. The technique, now known as *high-level data link control (HDLC)*, was designed to make the protocol independent of the many different encoding formats and control sequences used. Using HDLC there is no necessity for the length of each character to be specified since the bit representation of the data, be it characters, binary numbers, decimal numbers or anything else, is contained wholly within the data field of the frame.

The header and trailer fields effectively delimit the data. The start of the frame is indicated by a unique flag sequence.

Since there are no preconceived notions of the structure of the data contained in the frame the protocol is often said to be *bit-oriented* to distinguish it from the character-oriented protocols described earlier.

HDLC is suitable for half-duplex or full-duplex synchronous transmission. Full-duplex means that the device and medium can both send and receive at the same time. Half-duplex describes the type of information flow which can be in either direction, but not both simultaneously. *Simplex* transmission is unusual in computer networks, but it means that information can flow only in one direction, for example, ordinary broadcast radio and television programmes.

There are three basic components of HDLC: (1) the frame structure, (2) the elements of procedure, and (3) the classes of procedure.

The frame structure is illustrated in figure 4.4. The data being transmitted are placed in the information field of the HDLC frame and are

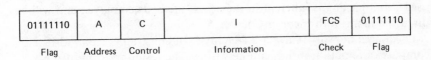

01111110	A	C	I	FCS	01111110
Flag	Address	Control	Information	Check	Flag

Figure 4.4 HDLC frame structure (FCS = frame check sequence)

surrounded by the control fields shown. The frame itself is delimited by two flag fields which have the special bit sequence shown. In order to prevent these fields from occurring in normal data and being interpreted as frame delimiters a technique known as *bit-stuffing* is employed. Thus, a zero bit is inserted by the sender after five consecutive one bits occurring in the remainder of the frame. The receiver performs the reverse function on the frame before passing the data on to the destination device or program. The use of a rigid frame structure, together with this transparency technique, avoids the need to scan the incoming data for control characters.

The address and control fields of the frame can be used to indicate the source or destination addresses and the purpose of the frame, depending on the circumstances in which it is being used. The frame check sequence (FCS) field is used for detecting errors that occur in the address control and information fields.

The 'elements of procedure' of HDLC specify the commands and responses used for data transfer. The 'classes of procedure' specify the sets of commands and responses appropriate to different modes of operation of the link (for example, master-slave, point-to-point, etc). More details of HDLC and other data link protocols can be found in reference [5].

The HDLC technique is much more flexible and efficient than the earlier data link protocols. It has become the basis for packet-switched networks and is also used in a modified form in several local area networks, for the reason that each frame of information can be separately addressed and interleaved with others from different senders to other addresses. This ability to share channel capacity between many different source and destination devices is the key to constructing a shared network offering unrestricted interconnections between users.

4.2 LOCAL AREA NETWORK TRANSMISSION TECHNIQUES

Designers of local area networks have taken the two basic requirements of multiplexing and the need for a reliable data-transmission service, which are common to all computer networks, and implemented them in an entirely novel way. This section is concerned with the data-transmission techniques used. Multiplexing is inherent in the access methods employed and will be discussed along with them in Chapter 5.

Local area networks have a different set of constraints from normal computer and data-transmission networks. The resulting form of the network follows largely from these constraints. Briefly the major considerations for local area networks are

- cheapness, compared with the cost of the attached devices,
- short distances, implying that simple modulation techniques can be used,
- simple interfaces can be used because of the short distances and simple
- modulation techniques used,
- the network cable is shared by all the users, so must be capable of
- supporting high transmission speeds,
- error rates must be low, which allows simpler interface devices.

It is not a straightforward matter to trade off the various requirements and produce a network that is suitable for all modes of use while still meeting all the design criteria, especially when one of them is simplicity. Local area networks have had one big advantage over many other systems in that, because they are wholly contained within one site, they can be designed and tuned to meet the particular requirements of the users on that site and are free from the constraints and regulations imposed by public telecommunications authorities.

A few broad ideas have been developed for local area networks which form a good basis for an examination of the techniques involved: (1) baseband signalling, (2) broadband signalling, (3) bus topology, and (4) ring topology.

Topologies were the subject of Chapter 3, so they will not be treated in much detail here.

4.2.1 Baseband

Baseband signalling literally means that the signal is not modulated at all. Thus the signal is either on the network or not. When considering digital data transmission the zero and one bits are given discrete values and the signal appears directly as those values on the network, and not as shifts of frequency, phase or amplitude on a high-frequency carrier wave.

Baseband techniques have been widely adopted by local area network designers because no modems are needed and the signal can be transmitted at high speed. Without special precautions they are not suitable for long-distance transmissions. They are also unsuited to circuits that are subject to noise, interference or random errors. In the restricted environment of a local area network, however, baseband signalling is often very suitable. The design of the interface devices, which take the place of modems, can be relatively simple since all they have to do is detect a changing signal.

In practical systems a technique known as *Manchester encoding* is used. This is a special form of baseband signalling that has the characteristic of transmitting distinct levels of signal to represent binary digits, but with additional features to allow strings of the same digit to be transmitted in such a manner that the receiver can distinguish the start and finish of each one.

Figure 4.5 shows a signal transmitted using Manchester encoding. The time interval needed for each digit is divided into two and during the first half the complement of the digit is transmitted. The second half is used to transmit the uncomplemented value. Thus a 1 bit is transmitted as a 0 followed by a 1. A 0 bit is a 1 followed by a 0. During each bit interval the signal changes midway so that the receiving and sending devices can always remain in step. The technique is said to be *self-clocking*. Manchester

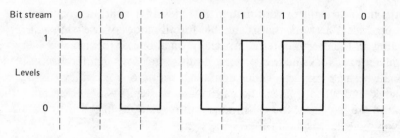

Figure 4.5 Manchester encoding

encoding is very easy to implement in practice, which in turn means that the interface devices and repeaters on the network can be made cheap and simple.

On a baseband network the absence of a transmission is indicated by a lack of any signal on the medium. If a device were to start transmission with the beginning of its data, then the listening devices would probably lose the first few bits because they need a finite time to lock on to the signal and adjust their internal clocks to the frequency of the sender. For this reason some networks precede transmissions by a short preamble consisting of a set bit sequence which ends in a particular manner. If the listener misses the start of the preamble it is still able to recognise the end by the appearance of this special sequence. After the preamble the data proper start. Ring-based systems do not usually need this preamble since data or idle characters circulate continuously.

If we compare this with the transmission of an HDLC frame, there are some similarities and differences. The header and trailer of an HDLC frame is a special unique bit sequence. At the end the receiver expects either the start of the data fields or the transmission of another header field. The preamble needed by some local area networks can take the place of the header, since it performs the same function. The trailer can be dispensed with altogether since the cessation of the signal indicates that the frame has ended. If the transmission ended prematurely the length of the frame would not match with the length field (if one is used), or the error-checking fields that are expected at the end would give incorrect results.

As mentioned earlier, baseband signalling is primarily suited to short-distance transmissions. The medium itself must be capable of changing state rapidly enough to carry the data. If the transmission speed is 10 Mbps and Manchester encoding is used, then the medium must be able to change state at least 20 million times per second. Not only must the medium be capable of transmitting information reliably at this speed, but the interfacing devices and repeaters must also be able to read and to transmit at this rate.

A channel operating in baseband mode effectively uses the whole bandwidth, so only one signal can be carried at any one time. With high-speed transmissions, short distances and data devices this is not a great disadvantage. Transmission of long duration streams of information could effectively lock out every other user.

4.2.2 Broadband

Broadband signalling is a more traditional technique of using wideband transmission circuits than baseband described in the previous section. Basically the technique modulates information on to analogue carrier waves. Since the media used have a very wide bandwidth (300–400 MHz), several frequencies of carrier wave can share the same physical circuits, so the medium can use frequency-division multiplexing techniques to share the circuit capacity. Although the same physical network is used by everybody, it has the appearance of several separate networks.

The technique has been used for some time by the providers of cable television circuits. In these several television channels are broadcast along a single piece of cable. Each channel is allocated a particular frequency and the receivers that are plugged into the cable tune in to the frequency appropriate to the channel that they want to see. A colour television channel requires a band 6–8 MHz wide to transmit all the information, so the channels on a cable television system are spaced 6–8 MHz apart. This includes the gaps, or guard bands, used between adjacent channels to minimise interference.

When broadband systems are used for data, modems are required to modulate the digital information on to a carrier wave. The bandwidth required depends on the rate at which the data are being transmitted, but practical implementations use 300 KHz (including guard bands) to transmit data at 128 Kbps. Higher transmission rates require wider bands. A typical division of frequencies in a local network is shown in figure 4.6.

Brief consideration of the implementations of a broadband system shows that there are a number of problems that need to be overcome.

The first point concerns the fact that, although the same physical network is used by all, the channels on it are logically separate. This may seem to be a positive advantage but it does have problems for a computer network. A device attached to the network is given a specific frequency band that it can use for transmission. The other device involved which is to receive the data transmitted by the first must tune in to that same frequency. For transmission in the other direction another frequency is needed. Thus, the modems used for this mode of use are a complementary pair, the transmit channel of one being the receiver channel of the other.

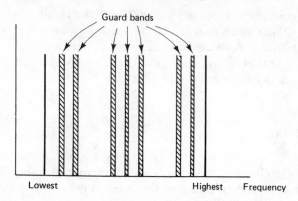

Figure 4.6 Frequency division of a broadband network

This system is acceptable for point-to-point links between pairs of devices, terminals to a computer for example. When a large number of terminals or other devices are involved the computer will be swamped with modems since each separate pair of channels requires a separate modem. The modems used for broadband networks are in effect radio-frequency (RF) transmitter/receivers as well as modulators/demodulators, and are thus rather complex items of equipment. Until recently each RF modem could operate on only one or two frequencies so it was difficult to set up links to other devices which used another frequency.

One solution to this problem is to employ what are known as *frequency-agile modems.* These are standard RF modems but with the ability to change easily from one frequency to another. They have to be told what frequency to use and then they change to it. One way of doing this is to incorporate a controller in the network. Whenever one device wishes to transmit to another (say a computer) it first transmits a 'call request' message to the controller on a frequency reserved for this purpose. The controller then scans its tables to find which frequencies are not in use and sends a message to the transmitter and receiver telling them which to switch to. The frequency-agile modems change to that pair of frequencies and from then until the end of the conversation only that pair of modems use these channels.

As an example of how the single broadband bus system would be used let us consider the process-control system illustrated in figure 4.7a. This shows the logical interconnection of the devices that are associated with monitoring and control, and the central controlling computer. How this can be implemented using a broadband bus is shown in figure 4.7b.

The controlling computer uses several of its input/output ports to connect to modems which are tuned to separate channels represented by A, B, C . . . Corresponding modems are used to connect the sensing and

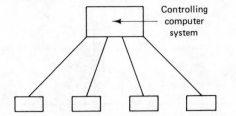

Controlling and monitoring devices (sensors, terminals, computers, etc.)

(a)

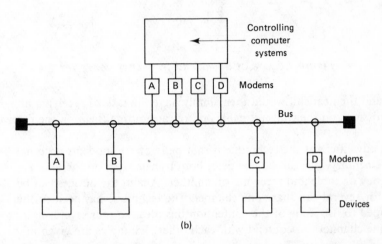

(b)

Figure 4.7 Using a broadband bus network. (a) Schematic view of a process control and monitoring system. (b) Actual implementation using a bus

monitoring devices to the bus. As can be seen the network wiring is simplified.

Another way of using a broadband bus which is becoming more popular is illustrated in figure 4.8. At one end of the bus is placed a special device called a *headend* which converts the whole set of frequencies used to transmit information into another set of frequencies which are used only for receiving. For example, if the total bandwidth of the medium is 300 MHz, lying between 100 MHz and 400 MHz, then the 100–250 MHz band could be allocated to the transmitted information. The headend would take each individual channel in this band, say that around 150 MHz, and convert it to a new frequency, 150 + 150 = 300 MHz, and retransmit it. All the modems listen to frequencies in the 250–400 MHz band.

A simpler method is to employ two cables, one for transmitting and the other for receiving. The same frequency would probably be used on each

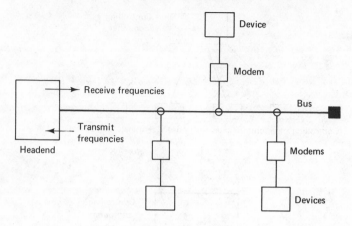

Figure 4.8 Use of a headend frequency converter

cable and the headend would then simply have the task of receiving all
transmissions on the transmit cable and retransmitting them on the receive
cable.

The advantage of the technique is that pairs of RF modems need not be
complementary, but can be identical, both transmitting on the one
frequency or cable and receiving on another. Again, the devices can be
paired or several can share one channel. The technique has been further
developed to use some of the contention bus ideas so that several users on
the same channel can contend with each other. Examples are given in
Chapter 6.

4.3 TRANSMISSION MEDIA

Any physical medium that is capable of carrying information in an electromagnetic form is potentially suitable for use on a local area network. In
practical systems the media used are generally twisted-pair cable, coaxial
cable and optical fibre. Radio, infra-red, microwave and laser technologies
are possible choices for special circumstances.

4.3.1 Twisted Pair

Twisted-pair cable is that normally used for standard telephones or telex
terminals. One or more pairs of cable are enclosed within a single outer

sheath. Each pair is twisted together in the form of a helix which results in fairly constant and predictable electrical characteristics.

Twisted-pair cable is generally used for analogue signals but has been successfully used for digital transmissions, especially in ring networks where the attenuation and imbalance between pairs can be corrected by the frequent use of repeaters. Because it is very difficult to guarantee that the lengths of individual wires in the pairs are exactly the same, differences in propagation times over long distances can become significant. Twisted-pair cable is normally used in a baseband mode, two or more pairs being used to signal the data being transmitted.

Different lengths of cable will mean that the signals being received will appear out of phase, so the repeaters will not be able to read the information accurately. For this reason the repeaters in a ring that uses twisted-pair cables are usually placed close together.

The actual bandwidth that can be carried by twisted-pair cables is remarkably high considering the fact that they were designed for analogue telephone traffic. It is possible to transmit data at up to 100 Mbps, although 10 Mbps is much more common.

Unless the cable is heavily shielded it is susceptible to electromagnetic interference from electrical machinery. For this reason it is considered unsuitable for use in manufacturing plants. For most circumstances it is adequate. Because twisted-pair cable is mainly used in rings, and in rings the repeater provides the point where another type of cable can be used, it is easy to insert a section of cable that is immune to interference in critical sections. Thus the ring can use twisted-pair cable for most of its length, with coaxial cable or even optical fibre for some other sections.

4.3.2 Coaxial Cable

Coaxial cable consists of a central conductor around which is a layer of insulating material separating it from a conducting shield, which in turn is covered by another insulating layer. The shield can be either a solid cylinder of metal or one or more layers of braided wire.

Coaxial cable is available in a wide variety of qualities, each of which has specific characteristics. Some are much better at transmitting high frequencies than others, or have very low attenuation, or high immunity to interference, etc. The highest quality cable is quite stiff and can be difficult to install, but low quality cable may be unsuitable for very high transmission speeds over long distances. Another variable feature of coaxial cable is its characteristic impedance at various frequencies. In most cases the impedence is 50 or 75 ohm at the normal range of operating frequencies.

Coaxial cable exhibits some desirable electrical characteristics which make it very unsuitable for many purposes. It is suitable for transmitting high-frequency signals while remaining relatively immune to electrical interference. It is suitable for both baseband and broadband use. Indeed cable television networks use coaxial cable that has a bandwidth of more than 300 MHz and yet is cheap to buy and can carry the signal over a wide area.

Used in the baseband model coaxial cable can easily transmit information at 10 Mbps, the limit being imposed more by the access methods used, the length of the cable involved and the transmitter/receivers used to drive the cable rather than the cable itself.

 Coaxial cable is also easy to cut and tap into without affecting its electrical characteristics. Thus, although it costs more than twisted-pair cable, the simpler installation and better electrical characteristics have made it the choice for most local area networks.

4.3.3 Optical Fibres

Optical fibres transmit light or infra-red rays instead of electrical signals. The cable consists of a filament of silica or plastic for transmitting the light, around which is another substance that has a lower refractive index to make the rays reflect internally and so minimise transmission losses.

The principle of light transmission through glass has been known for a long time, but it is only in the past 10 or 15 years that long optical fibre cables have become available offering the bandwidth and low attenuation suitable for data transmission. The cables obviously vary widely in quality but it is possible to obtain cable capable of transmitting 50 Mbps over several kilometres without the need for repeaters.

Data to be transmitted through an optical fibre cable are converted to light pulses by a light-emitting diode or an injection-laser diode. The light so produced is directed down one end of the cable, as shown in figure 4.9. At the other end of the length of cable a photodiode detector picks up the light pulses and converts them into electrical pulses. These are amplified, reshaped and made available to the attached device before being converted back into light by a light source for transmission over the next section.

Optical fibre cables are more expensive than ordinary electrical cables, and they are much more difficult to connect to since the light source has to shine directly down the cable. The repeaters are also complex devices since they have the task of converting light into electrical signals and vice versa, as well as amplifying the signal, etc. For these reasons optical fibres are not frequently used in local area networks. Their great value is for long-distance links or for areas where electrical interference is a problem, since they are completely immune to the latter.

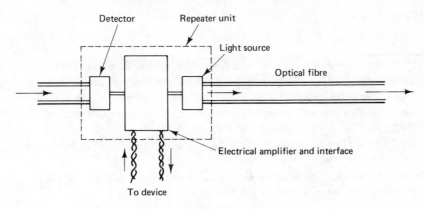

Figure 4.9 Optical fibre data transmission

Optical fibres are essentially one-way transmission media with a source at one end and a detector at the other. Two-way transmission requires that two cables be used. Given this fact, optical fibres are ideal for ring networks where information always flows in the same direction.

4.3.4 Other Media

Radio transmission can be used for carrying data, but in the context of local area networks it is not really a valid alternative to cables. It is relevant when two or more local networks need to be linked, especially if the rate of data flow between them needs to be high. Ordinary telephone circuits are generally unsuitable for this but radio transmissions can have the bandwidth required.

Infra-red radiation is a possible medium for use within a single room, especially an open-plan office. An infra-red transmitter/receiver would be placed within 'sight' of all the terminals on other devices which would themselves incorporate infra-red transmitter/receivers. Transmissions would be to and from the main infra-red repeater in the room which would in turn be connected to the rest of the network elsewhere on the site. The technique has advantages in open-plan offices where trailing cables can be a nuisance or even dangerous, and where access to cable ducts is often difficult. It is unobtrusive and easy to install and has sufficient bandwidth for most purposes.

Infra-red, visible light and microwaves offer real possibilities of communications between buildings that are within sight of one another.

52 *Introduction to Local Area Computer Networks*

REFERENCES

1 Cole, R., *Computer Communications*, Macmillan, London, 1982.
2 Tanenbaum, A. S., *Computer Networks*, Prentice-Hall Inc., Englewood Cliffs, New Jersey, 1981.
3 *Handbook of Data Communications*, NCC Publications, Manchester, 1982.
4 Scott, P. R. D., *Modems in Data Communications*, NCC Publications, Manchester, 1980.
5 Scott, P. R. D., *Introducing Data Communications Standards*, NCC Publications, Manchester, 1979.

5 Software and Hardware Requirements

Underlying every network is the physical transmission medium: the wire, optical fibre, radio transmission or whatever other medium has been chosen. The nodes in the network are linked together, using the medium, into the network topology. Previous chapters have examined the physical media and network topologies that are suitable for local area networks, but how they are used in practice has not yet been described. This chapter is concerned with explaining how the topology and physical media that make up the network can be made to perform in a manner useful to the end-user.

At least four functions must be performed by the network and the devices using it

Signal transmissions How to place the data on to the network in such a manner that it can be transmitted to other locations.

Network sharing How to allocate a share of the total bandwidth of the network among all the users.

Data framing How the messages are blocked up into manageable sizes in a standard way for transmission.

Addressing How to ensure that a message for one particular device does not get lost and reaches only the chosen recipient(s).

Naturally, for the network to perform properly the same techniques must be used by every device on it.

Deciding on the best techniques for any situation involves weighing the advantages of one method against its disadvantages in certain circumstances. Some topologies and access methods are more suitable for some applications than others.

The access method itself is one of the most important aspects of local area network design. It is often software-controlled, or implemented in firmware. The media used and the topology of the network are less critical from the end-user's point of view.

Data-transmission services are needed to detect and to correct transmission errors, to address other users uniquely, to packet up the data in the form required by the access method, and so on. The end-user of a network will need to use extra services built on top to obtain a network with the quality required.

5.1 CONNECTION REQUIREMENTS

Regardless of the topology, in order to use a cable or other physical transmission medium in a network, it is first necessary to connect a transmitter/receiver to it and then provide a range of functions and rules to enable the medium to be used to form a network. Figure 5.1 shows the major components at a connection to the medium.

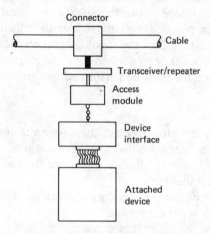

Figure 5.1 Connecting to a local area network cable

We shall assume that we have a physical medium which is suitable for the purposes intended (that is, it has the required data-transmission rate, topology, etc.). The first step towards making this into a useful network is to provide a signalling device to transmit and to receive the data signals, and a way of connecting it to the medium.

The connector can be either a passive or an active device. A passive connector performs no network functions other than transmitting and receiving signals for the devices it serves. An active connector performs these functions, but in addition it is also involved in signal transmissions between other devices on the network. A passive connector can be removed from the network without affecting transmissions between other users; an active connector cannot.

A passive connector is typically used in broadcast networks, because in these the signals representing the information are transmitted once into the network and then allowed to die away naturally. The connector is in effect similar to a radio transmitter or receiver. In most practical local area networks the physical medium used will be a cable rather than the radio airwaves. The connector will thus be some sort of device that can make electrical contact with the conductors in the cable. Figure 5.2 shows one possible method of making a connection to a coaxial cable. This is the sort

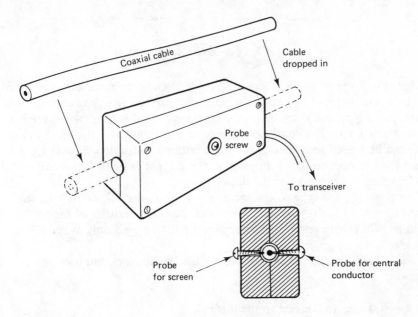

Figure 5.2 Coaxial cable connector that does not require the cable to be cut

of connector that can be used in situations where it is unnecessary or undesirable actually to cut the cable in order to make contact. The cable itself is pierced by two probes, one of which makes contact with the outer metal shield, the other piercing the shield and dielectric layers to reach the inner core. The actual transmitter/receiver (usually called a *transceiver*) is connected to the terminals of this connector. Alternatively, the cable can be cut and an ordinary T connection inserted.

Another form of connector is shown in figure 5.3. In this the cable is cut and ordinary coaxial connectors are attached to the free ends. These are plugged into corresponding sockets on the transceiver. By this means it is claimed that a better connection can be made in the cable.

Naturally, a truly passive connector should be completely invisible electrically to the network as a whole, but in practice this is impossible to

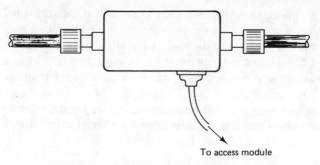

To access module

Figure 5.3 Plug-in coaxial cable connector

achieve with cable media. Thus the passive connectors are usually restricted as to where they can be placed on the cable (depending on the transmission rate, cable type, etc.), and as to the maximum number that can be used on a single segment. The combined connector and transceiver shown in figure 5.3 can be placed anywhere in the cable without restriction. It uses special balancing circuits so that transmission characteristics of the cable are not affected by the presence of the device.

Surprisingly, the type of connector shown in figure 5.2, when used in conjunction with a transceiver, does alter the characteristics of the medium and to help ensure reliable transmission it must be used only at specific intervals.

The advantages of passive connectors for the designer and user of a network are

- they are easy to connect to the medium,
- non-disruptive devices can be employed,
- they can be cheap if few electronic components are used,
- since they can be cheap, more can be provided when the network is installed, thus making it easy to connect new devices, move others around, etc.

Disadvantages are

- they are less reliable under adverse conditions,
- the network size and cable segment length are limited to the range of the transmitter, since the connector does not amplify the signals for other users further along the network.

Alternatives to completely passive connectors, and in some circumstances a necessity, are active devices. The characteristic of an active connector is that it cannot be removed from the network without affecting the operation of the network as a whole, as well as affecting the device that uses it to access the medium. Active connectors are generally essential for ring-shaped networks since the signal is not normally permitted to disappear naturally after each transmission, but instead must be continuously regenerated. Connectors that perform the task of allowing the attached device to send and receive the signals travelling round the network are usually employed to amplify and regenerate the signals as well.

Figure 5.4 shows the form of a typical ring repeater which is inserted in series with the cable. Since most rings send signals in one direction only, the repeater can consist of a receiving section, a section to regenerate the signal and provide a mechanism for inserting new packets of data, etc., and a transmitter to send the signal to the next repeater.

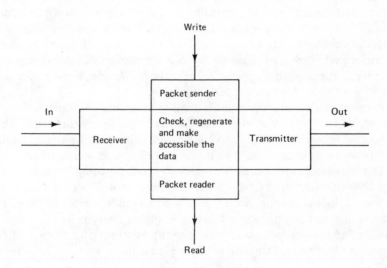

Figure 5.4 Ring repeater functions

The most obvious advantages of this approach are

- since signals can be regenerated at each repeater the network can be long and not limited by the transmitting power of individual repeaters,
- the quality of the transmission medium does not need to be very high,
- each repeater can check the integrity of the data passing through it,
- it provides a flexible means to access and control the network,
- the incoming transmission medium can be different from the outgoing medium.

Disadvantages include

- transmission speed for the whole network can be slowed down by passage through the repeater,
- failure of a repeater requires it to be bypassed or replaced for the network to continue to operate,
- it is necessary actually to break the physical medium to insert a repeater, although this can be achieved with minimum disruption using jack sockets.

The transceiver or repeater has to perform certain functions for the attached device, but these vary from one access method or implementation to another. Their main function common to all systems is to listen to transmissions on the network and make them available to the other devices connected to the network, in particular the access module shown in figure 5.1. The transceiver itself is not usually responsible for deciding which packets of data are addressed to it, or how to perform the access protocol. The transceiver or repeater also serves to place packets of information on the network for onward transmission to their destination, having been given them in the correct format, properly addressed.

To ensure that receivers can understand the information transmitted, the sending and receiving transceivers or repeaters must be synchronised. This is achieved by means of special clocking signals, either sent separately from the data or incorporated into it as in the Manchester encoding scheme.

If the broadband method of transmission is employed by the network (see Chapter 4) the transceivers are modems, sometimes with special functions to perform additional channel access. Baseband coupling devices are generally much simpler and can operate efficiently at higher transmission speeds, because all they need to do is to recognise the existence of a signal and distinguish the digits rather than modulate these on to a carrier as well.

5.2 ACCESS METHODS

The bulk of this chapter is devoted to the access techniques used for local area networks. In fact a very large number of different access methods have been proposed and tried at one time or another, but only a handful have been retained in common use.

In this chapter only the techniques that have been the most influential on existing systems will be considered in any detail. Readers interested in other experimental techniques are advised to consult references [1–3] in the first instance, where they will find many more techniques presented together with additional references to more detailed descriptions.

A local area network is just one example of a shared resource, although it is the network itself that is being shared rather than something like a printer that is attached to it. In Chapter 4 various ways of sharing the capacity of a transmission channel were discussed, based on normal multiplexing and polling techniques. In its broadest sense time-division multiplexing is one way of allocating a channel to a group of separate devices so that, at any one instant, only one device is using it. No assumption is made in this statement concerning the methods employed to divide up the time among the devices or the length of time allowed for each. Frequency-division multiplexing is an alternative technique employed for media or networks that are capable of handling more than one channel at a time on different frequency bands.

Both time-division and frequency-division multiplexing techniques are applied successfully to local area networks, but several novel adaptations of them have been made to suit the very different requirements of the different media, topologies and modes of use. Local area networks seldom employ a central time-division multiplexer or concentrator to allocate the network capacity, as they would if they used the technique in the normal way. Instead the responsibility for allocating the network capacity is usually distributed among all the access points (or *stations*) on the network. Frequency-division multiplexing cannot be handled so easily by distributing control, so the frequencies on which the devices are allowed to operate are allocated by a network supervisor, or by a controlling device in the more sophisticated systems.

A convenient way of dividing up local area network access methods for the purposes of description is to treat ring and broadcast-bus access techniques separately. Only those techniques based on time-division multiplexing will be considered in detail since the frequency-division multiplexing methods used on the broadband bus networks have already been covered in sufficient detail in Chapter 4. Here it is sufficient to note that the broadband bus systems employ standard frequency-division techniques to allocate separate channels. Within these channels the time-division multiplexing techniques about to be described are often employed, thereby providing for interconnection between several devices within a frequency band independent of communications in other bands.

5.2.1 Ring and Loop Systems

Local area networks in the shape of rings or loops, in which information passes sequentially round in one direction are potentially easier to control than broadcast-bus systems, so they will be dealt with first. The information and flow of control usually pass round a ring from one access point, or station, to another. When each station has the packet of data passed to it, it is then in a position to read it, remove it, retransmit it, alter it or add a new packet of its own. This explicit method of handing control from one station to the next makes it easy to devise fool-proof methods of use.

A loop is even easier to control than a ring since the loop controller has explicit control of the flow of control and information. Since the loop is of limited importance in local area networks designed to interconnect numbers of independent devices, the methods particular to loops will be discussed only briefly.

A ring network can be thought of as one large 'distributed multiplexer and transmission system combined. The techniques used for accessing the ring ensure that the available time is divided up among all the users of the network.

Rings and loops are generally accessed through a repeater which receives the data packet passed to it by the preceding repeater, makes it available to the attached device, allows the device to transmit information, and transmits the packet to the next repeater. Repeaters are usually designed to operate as quickly as possible so that they do not hold up data transmission unnecessarily, especially when they are not directly involved in sending or receiving information.

Reference [3] gives a good description of many ring access techniques that have been proposed.

5.2.1.1 Loop Access Techniques

Loop networks are usually short and serve a small number of terminals. They are generally developments of the traditional form of the shared multipoint line system for sharing line capacity, and as such they operate in a similar manner.

One common way of operating a loop is for the controller to poll each device individually. If the polled device has a data packet to send it does so, and the controller receives it and if necessary passes it on to another part of the network. If the controller is sending a data packet to a device on the loop, it addresses the packet to that device; all the others ignore it.

Another way of using a loop, more suitable for devices that need to send data intermittently, is for an empty packet to be sent out by the controller. Any device with data to send can put them in the empty packet. Once a packet is filled it is rendered inaccessible to the other users on the loop. A single device that is outputting data at a high rate could easily lock out the devices that follow it on the loop by using this method.

Loop techniques are especially suitable for small numbers of low-usage devices spread over a small area. Loop implementations can be configured in such a way that data can flow in either direction, although only one way at a time. If the loop is broken, then the two parts can still operate independently, provided that the controller is able to handle them.

5.2.1.2 Register or Buffer Insertion

Register or buffer insertion is one technique that is particularly suited to ring-shaped local area networks. It operates in the following manner. When a device has information to send it stores it in a shift register. This register can be connected into a circuit in series; data are then fed into one end, shifted through the register and output from the other end, as shown in figure 5.5a, b.

Used in a ring the register is switched in series with the remainder of the ring whenever there is a convenient gap between other packets travelling round. The register stays in series with the ring and all the packets of data are diverted through the register (figure 5.5c). When the packet originally transmitted by the device at that location returns to it and is completely

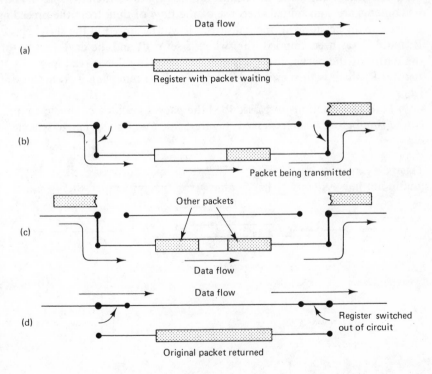

Figure 5.5 Idealised register insertion

stored in the register (figure 5.5d), the register is switched out of the circuit. In principle the operation is easy to envisage, but in practice it is more complex since the speed at which the register is switched in and out must be adequate, and the destination device must also be able to read the data and, preferably, flag that they have been received.

A more practical situation is shown diagrammatically in figure 5.6. In this implementation two registers are used: one to transmit, and one to

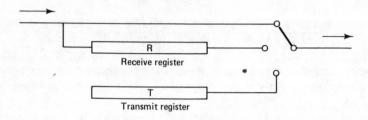

Figure 5.6 Practical register insertion scheme

receive. When the device has a packet to send it to places it in register T. At a convenient gap between packets on the ring the switch is set to T and its contents are transmitted. Because of the flow of data from the preceding device cannot be stopped, the data from it will be stored in the shift register R. Once T has been emptied, the switch is set to R and the device waits for the return of the packet just transmitted. Eventually this is read into register R which is then switched out of circuit so removing it from the ring.

In both the situations just described the packet makes a complete circuit of the ring before being removed. Figure 5.7 shows an alternative scheme

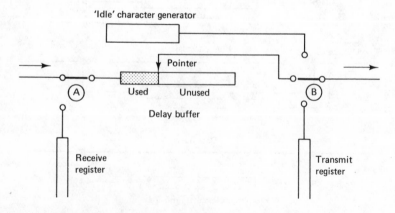

Figure 5.7 Alternative practical register insertion scheme

which permits the packet to be removed by the destination device. This is difficult to achieve satisfactorily with the schemes shown in figures 5.5 and 5.6 because the transmitting device still has a register inserted in series with the ring and needs something (the packet it sent) to make ti remove the register. The system in figure 5.7 uses three registers, two switches and a device for generating 'idle' signals. It works in the following way.

The ring is generally in series with a delay buffer which has a movable pointer. At the start of operation this buffer is empty and the pointer is at the left-hand (zero) end. Data travelling around the ring effectively bypass this buffer. When the device has a packet to transmit this is loaded into the transmit register and, when there is a gap in packets on the ring, switch B is moved to the transmit register and its contents are transmitted. At this instant, incoming data are stored in the delay buffer (itself a shift register) and the pointer is moved along to mark the end of the data. If the incoming characters are 'idle' characters, representing no data, these are not stored but the pointer is stepped back towards zero. When the transmit buffer is empty, switch B is set to the delay buffer and the pointer ceases to move.

The destination device for a packet recognises that it is addressed to it by the header and switches A to the receive register. The incoming data are read into this register, and at the end of the packet the switch A is set back to the input of the delay buffer. During this time, while a packet is being read into the receive register, the ring continues to operate by means of the delay buffer and/or the 'idle' character generator continuing to transmit.

When the pointer in the delay buffer is at the zero position, switch B takes 'idle' characters from the generator.

In this last example, if a sender receives back a packet which it transmitted itself, it knows that the destination did not read it for some reason. If the packet is removed, then the destination device must have read it into its receive buffer. An extra level of protocol is generally needed to handle packets that have been damaged in transit.

5.2.1.3 Empty Slot Technique

The empty slot method of operating a ring does not depend on the use of shift registers and high-speed switches in the repeaters or attached devices. One or more skeleton packets or slots circulate continuously round the ring. Their number never changes and is determined by the length of the slot, the total length of the ring, and by the ring startup procedure. If the ring is very short, either short slots must be used, their number restricted, or a delay buffer inserted somewhere in the ring; otherwise, the beginning of the slot would return to the sender before the end had been transmitted. For this reason, many practical implementations of empty slot rings employ only one short slot and a delay buffer.

At ring start-up, one repeater or device generates a slot and sends it round the ring. If it returns to the sender, then the ring must be complete and it can begin operation.

When a device has information to transmit, it loads it into a buffer or register and waits until the repeater immediately preceding it passes an empty slot to it. The slot can be recognised as empty by the control field in the header. The device or repeater does not attempt to store the slot (this would slow down the ring too much), but shifts the data packet from its buffer into the data fields of the slot as it is passed through the repeater, after first setting the full/empty flag to 'full' and placing the destination address in the header. The slot continues round the ring, as shown in figure 5.8, until it reaches the destination device whose repeater reads the information into its own buffers without clearing the slot. (It cannot clear the slot because the full/empty flag must be at the head of the slot, and this will have been passed on before the repeater reads the address field.) Optionally, depending on the implementation, a flag at the end of the slot is set by the destination, to indicate that the packet was received.

The slot (still flagged 'full') is then passed from repeater to repeater until it returns to its sender. The sending device knows that it sent out this packet, by counting the number of slots on the ring, and so it sets the full/empty flag back to 'empty', thereby allowing it to be used by another device. If the slot carries an acknowledgement field, the sender checks it to find out if the destination received the packet.

In one form the technique does not require the sender to mark the slot as 'empty' on its return if it wants to use it again. This would allow it to retain one slot for as long as it liked. In rings with only one slot in use this would obviously be unfair, so most implementations insist that the slot is emptied after one complete revolution. In this manner the opportunity to use the slot is passed sequentially from one device to another.

If the destination device is not listening, is unable to read the packet, or the slot is in error, this fact can be flagged to the sender using the acknowledgement field. The sender can then retransmit the packet in the next free slot. Thus, despite the apparent waste of time caused by the full slot making one complete circuit, it is in fact used both to carry data on the outward journey, and to receive an acknowledgement on the return.

If a slot that is being used is not removed by the sending device (possibly because of a failure in this device following transmission), the slot could continue to circulate marked 'full' indefinitely. In practice one of the devices or repeaters is given the responsibility of emptying slots that have passed it unchanged more than once. This task is usually given to a special device which is also responsible for starting the network and monitoring it for errors.

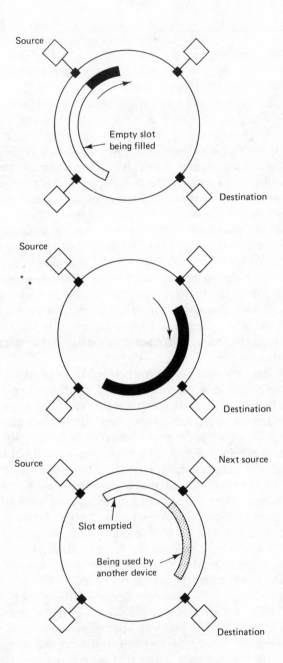

Figure 5.8 Empty slot ring

5.2.1.4 Token Passing

In the empty slot method of using a ring, control is passed implicitly together with an empty packet. An alternative solution is to use an explicit unique character sequence, called a token, which is passed round the ring. Whenever a device has data to transmit, it must wait for the preceding device to pass the token to it (figure 5.9).

When the device receives the token it temporarily removes it from the ring and places it behind the packet of data that it holds ready to transmit in a shift register. The transmit shift register is then switched into the outgoing side of the ring and its contents, with the token at the end, are sent into the ring. The register is then switched out of circuit and the device waits for the return of its packet. The first packet that it receives on the incoming side must, under normal circumstances, be the one that it sent out, so it reads it into a register for analysis and then switches the ring back into circuit in a similar manner to the register insertion technique. The device then awaits the token again if it has more data to transmit.

The incoming stream of a device that has just transmitted should always be headed by its own packet because each sender is responsible for removing its own from the string of packets. Since each packet transmitted is always the last one in the string before the token, the ones in front must reach their original senders first and thus be removed. In this scheme there is no need to divert the incoming stream into a delay buffer while a packet is being transmitted.

A destination device would normally operate like an empty slot repeater and just read the packet as it passed through, probably setting an acknowledgement flag in the trailer, but not otherwise altering it.

The major problems with token-passing rings are the loss of the token and the non-removal of a packet by the sender. The former situation could occur if a token was removed by a transmitting device and not replaced, perhaps because of a hardware failure, or because the token was damaged by a transmission error and became unrecognisable. A packet may not have been removed because the sending device failed in some manner and could not switch the incoming stream into the receive buffer. Either situation can be handled successfully by means of a special monitoring device that would recognise if a token was missing from the end of a data stream, or if a packet had already been circulated. In the former case a new token would be generated, and in the latter the packet removed.

In the absence of a special monitoring device a missing token can easily be handled by allowing each device or repeater to generate a new one if, after a random time interval, a token had not been received.

Duplicate tokens are also possible when two devices generate new ones simultaneously. However, if each device that generates a token always puts a full packet in front of it, and then checks that the first packet returned is

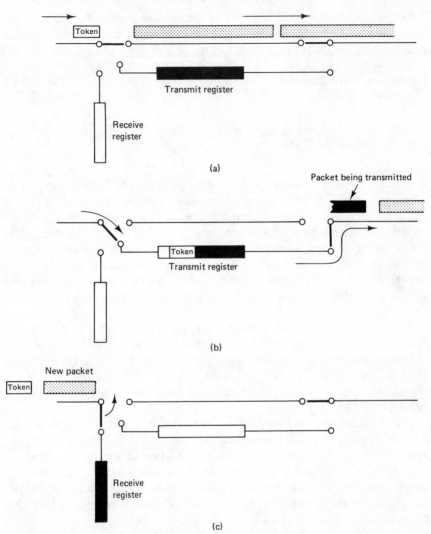

Figure 5.9 Token-passing ring. (a) Waiting for token. (b) Transmitting packet. (c) Removing packet

the same, the problem can be avoided. Each incoming packet is checked and discarded if it differs from the one transmitted. Two stations doing this simultaneously would remove each other's packets (and tokens). After a random time interval a new token would be generated somewhere in the ring. If each device that has just transmitted a packet always discards the first packets of the incoming string until it reaches its own, then the problem of unremoved packets is also easily handled.

Token passing is very efficient to implement and does not require a special monitoring device to the extent that the empty slot technique does. It does, however, require considerably more complex repeater hardware and control software at each of the devices in order to implement the register switching and token handling.

5.2.2 Broadcast-bus System

A broadcast system is one in which a message (or packet containing part of a message) is sent into the system and can be heard more or less simultaneously all over it. The signal rapidly dies away once the transmission has ceased. The essence of a broadcast system is the fact that all the users of it are capable of hearing everything transmitted, whether it is to them, to another user or to everybody. Thus some way of sharing the bus must be devised to allow a reasonable number of devices to use it for intercommunication. It is difficult to devise a fair method of sharing a communication channel.

There is one obvious way around this problem, and that is to allocate time slots to each device. This is the normal time-division multiplexing technique described earlier. It is not generally considered a useful technique for local area networks, because it is very inefficient unless every device is always ready to use its time slot when its turn comes round, and this does not happen often in practice.

The solutions generally adopted are in fact adaptations of statistical time-division multiplexing techniques, but with the control distributed to all the access points on the network, as mentioned earlier. In general terms the users with data to transmit do so whenever possible, the main problems arising when two or more decide to transmit at the same time. Many ways have been devised to overcome this conflict; all involve each device attached agreeing to abide by the rules for access laid down by the designer of the system. When two or more devices try to send at the same time there is contention on the network. Each device contends with all the others for use of the network.

When two packets of information are broadcast at the same time they are said to have collided, with the result that the information each contains is damaged or corrupted. A foolproof method of detecting collisions and corrupted packets is obviously needed to implement successfully this type of network. Having detected, or been informed of, a lost or corrupted packet, the devices involved must schedule that packet for retransmission in such a manner that it is unlikely to collide with the same packet that was involved in the original collision. This procedure is governed by the back-off algorithm.

Since a broadcast system is available to everyone with the correct transmitting and receiving equipment, an addressing scheme is also required to ensure that each device can identify information sent to it. In order to implement a suitable addressing scheme, to ensure a reasonably fair division of use of the network and to provide a convenient method of checking for corrupted or erroneous information, data are always placed in packets which may be fixed, or more usually variable, in size. The address of the destination is included in the header of the packet so that the destination device can read it into internal storage for subsequent processing; the other devices on the network can safely ignore it. The header usually contains the address of the sender, because there is no other way that the destination can find out from where the packet came, unless there is only one transmitter on the network, or some other unusual condition.

Having covered some of the basic principles common to all broadcast-bus systems, the different techniques can be described, beginning with the techniques devised for the wide area ALOHA network.

5.2.2.1 Pure ALOHA

The ALOHA network, from which this technique takes its name, is a radio broadcast network covering the Hawaiian islands which first began operation in 1970. Being neither a short-distance local area network, nor using a bus cable topology, it may be wondered why it should be considered in a book on local area networks at all. It is, however, a network that uses packets to send information and that relies on every user sharing the same transmission channel.

The purpose of the ALOHA network was to link the central computing system in Honolulu belonging to the University of Hawaii to terminals on all the islands in the group. Two radio-frequencies were allocated: one for computer-to-terminal broadcasts, and the other for terminal-to-computer messages. Since there is only one device transmitting on the first channel no difficulty is encountered; however all the terminals can transmit on the other channel, which is precisely the situation encountered in broadcast-bus local area networks.

A technique, now known as a *pure ALOHA*, was devised to enable all the terminals to share the channel to the computer centre. It is very simple in concept. Each terminal can only listen to the computer-to-terminal channel, so it has no way of knowing whether the terminal-to-computer channel is being used by any other terminal. Thus, when a terminal has a packet ready to send it transmits it regardless of whether the channel is currently in use or not. On completion of the transmission it starts an interval timer which it uses to decide if the packet was corrupted during transmission. If, after the time interval, it has not received an acknowledgement for that packet from the central computer it transmits it again, and restarts the timer. To reduce the possibility that the same packets will collide again, the interval is randomly generated.

The receiver at the central computer will hear either a normal uncollided packet or a damaged one. Every packet is checked against its error-checking field. If the packet has no errors, an acknowledgement is transmitted on the computer-to-terminal channel, therefore without fear of collision. If two or more packets collide, the result will be unintelligible, so no acknowledgements are sent.

The normal situation on the terminal-to-computer channel is shown diagrammatically in figure 5.10. In it two packets are shown colliding.

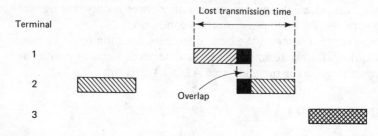

Figure 5.10 ALOHA terminal-to-computer channel usage

Although the amount that they overlap is very small, both packets are corrupted and must be retransmitted. The total time wasted on the channel is from the beginning of the first packet to be transmitted to the end of the last. This demonstrates the main problem with the pure ALOHA technique: poor channel utilisation when the load is heavy.

5.2.2.2 Slotted ALOHA

A simple way of improving the pure ALOHA technique is to restrict slightly the times when the terminal can transmit in order to reduce the total channel time wasted when packets collide. No other change is required in the network access and the transmitter still does not need to listen to the channel on which it is transmitting.

The whole time interval is split up by the central system into equal-length 'slots'. Each terminal is allowed to transmit only at the start of each slot. Thus the situation is similar to that shown in figure 5.11. When two devices decide to transmit at the same time they still transmit the whole of their packets, but they do so in a synchronised manner so that the time lost is limited to the width of the network time slot, as shown.

In this manner the total time wasted on the network is very much reduced and the efficiency of the system (36.8 per cent) is double that of the pure ALOHA technique.

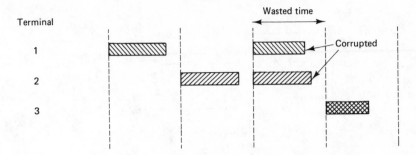

Figure 5.11 Slotted ALOHA channel usage

Although both pure and slotted ALOHA were designed for a very special purpose, using radio channels, the techniques can be applied to simple broadcast-bus local area networks. However, because of the relatively low efficiency, other methods have been devised, all of which require considerably more intelligence in all the devices attached, or in the interfaces between dumb terminals (for example) and the network.

5.2.2.3 Carrier-sense Multiple Access (CSMA)

One way of improving the overall efficiency of the pure and slotted ALOHA methods is to refrain from transmitting a packet if someone else is already doing so. This can easily be accomplished if the device that is ready to send listens to the channel before actually transmitting. If the channel is in use the device waits until the current transmission ceases and then makes its own transmission. However, a signal takes a finite time to reach all the extremities of the network, so it may happen that more than one device decides to transmit at the same instant. The signal from each of the devices will not reach the others until they too have started transmission, in which case all the packets in transit at that time are corrupted, as shown in figure 5.12.

In the straightforward form of this technique the sending devices do not continue to monitor the medium for other transmissions once their own has begun. Thus, even though the packets are being corrupted, they are still transmitted in their entirety. There will be no positive acknowledgements of safe receipt for the lost packets so, after a time-out period, the sending devices will realise that they were corrupted and will attempt to retransmit. In order to prevent the same packets from colliding again, most practical implementations wait a random time interval before attempting retransmission.

In *non-persistent CSMA*, devices that are waiting for an existing transmission to cease do not necessarily try to transmit their own packet as soon

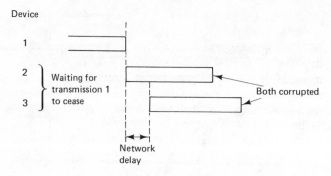

Figure 5.12 CSMA

as the network is quiet. If, however, the devices attempt to transmit at the first opportunity with a probability of *p*, then the method is called p-*persistent CSMA*. Thus, if *n* devices are waiting to transmit in a *p*-persistent implementation, then *n.p* devices will attempt it as soon as the channel becomes quiet. If $p = 1$, each device waiting to transmit will do so as soon as the existing transmission ceases. When two or more devices are waiting, their subsequent transmissions will collide and be lost. This situation occurs most often when the network is being heavily loaded. To minimise the quantity of data lost, a value of *p* less than unity is usually chosen. A high value of *p* reduces the time that the channel is likely to be quiet, whereas a low value reduces the likelihood of collisions. The optimum choice depends on many factors: the time taken for a transmission to reach all parts of the network, packet length, number of users waiting to transmit, etc. A good discussion of the problems can be found in reference [4].

Another way of scheduling transmissions using the CSMA technique is to allocate network-wide time slots and permit devices to start transmissions only at the beginning of a time slot. This is analogous to the slotted ALOHA method.

As a practical technique for local area networks CSMA in its slotted and *p*-persistent forms cannot compete with carrier sense multiple access with *collision detection*, which is considered next.

5.2.2.4 Carrier-sense Multiple Access with Collision Detection (CSMA/CD)

A major cause of inefficiency in both the ALOHA techniques and in ordinary CSMA is the fact that a complete packet is transmitted even though it is overlapping with another. In limited-distance networks the time taken for a signal to propagate to all parts of the network is very small compared with the time it takes to transmit a packet. Thus the period during which the network appears quiet, even though another device somewhere else on it is transmitting, is very short. During this time, known as the *collision window*, two or more packets may be transmitted which will ultimately collide and become corrupted.

A vast improvement can be made by first of all listening to the network for a transmission (*carrier sensing*) and then transmitting if it is quiet, but at the same time listening to the transmission (*collision detection*). Thus, if another packet is being transmitted elsewhere, the signal heard by all the transmitting devices will not match the information each is transmitting. The listening devices will also hear a confused jumble of signals. When each transmitter realises that its packet has collided it then ceases transmission to save wasting channel time. Since the collision window is short for networks that cover short distances (typical local area networks), the amount of time wasted is short compared with the length of a typical packet (figure 5.13).

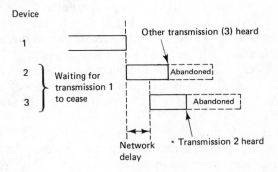

Figure 5.13 CSMA/CD

If a collision occurs, the devices involved cease transmission and try again some time later. In order to avoid the same packets colliding again, the time that each device waits before sensing the network again is random. It may happen that a packet being retransmitted collides again with another packet from another device. In this case the same procedure is followed, but the time it waits before attempting to retransmit is made longer. If, after a specific number of retries the transmission has still been unsuccessful, the device gives up the attempt and reports a possible error condition to its user. Thus, as the load on the network increases, so the rate of transmission of the individual devices reduces to match the capacity. As soon as the load is reduced the devices still transmitting immediately adjust.

CSMA/CD can be very efficient in practice, with well over 90 per cent of the available capacity of the channel being used, compared with 83 per cent for the optimum standard CSMA technique. The result is that CSMA/CD has been chosen as the basis for many practical local area network designs.

CSMA/CD does not require specific acknowledgements of individual packets for the sender to know that the packet was not corrupted in transmit. Obviously, this can cause problems if the destination of the packets is not listening for some reason. Less sophisticated techniques for using the channel would quickly detect that the listener did not respond and would therefore assume that the packets had failed to reach their destination or that the destination was unavailable. CSMA/CD requires the end devices to implement a higher level of protocol in order to ensure that acknowledgements are sent back to the sender whenever required.

5.2.2.5 Token Access

Another way of using the channel capacity of a broadcast-bus local area network is to reserve it in some way for a period of time, during which only one device can transmit. The standard time-division multiplexer does this for each of the devices attached to it, but in a rather inefficient way.

A better way is to use the token-passing technique. In this a special packet with a special easily recognisable bit sequence, called a token, is passed from device to device around the network. The token itself does not carry any information, but it is used to permit the holder of it to transmit information packets. Only one token is in existence on the network at any one time.

The way that the technique works is as follows (figure 5.14). The token is first of all created in some manner by a special device on the network, or by one of the devices connected to it. Once in existence it is passed by the holder to another device in some predetermined sequence (A to E to D, etc.). When a device is ready to transmit a packet of information, it waits until it is passed the token by the device before it in the sequence. Before it passes the token on to the next one it first transmits its packet of information (A to D, for example) which includes the address of the destination. The device (D) will read in the packet in the normal way. The sender will then transmit the token packet with the address field containing the address of the next device (E) in the sequence. This ensures that no two devices can transmit at the same instant and so no packets will be corrupted by colliding with others. The same device can be included more than once in the complete sequence (A is included twice in figure 5.14).

Two major implementation problems can be envisaged. The first concerns the token itself. If the token is sent to one device and that device does not read it, possibly because it is not working properly or not switched on, then the token disappears from the network. No device can transmit until it has the token so some procedure must be devised to ensure that a token is generated after an interval during which no packets have been transmitted. The token can either be generated by only one device, which is specifically

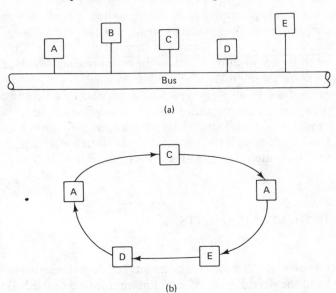

Figure 5.14 Token access technique on a bus. (a) Physical arrangement on bus. (b) Order in which devices get the token

given this task, or by any device. In the latter situation it is possible that more than one token could appear on the network. Some procedure must be devised to remove duplicates. To minimise this possibility when more than one device can regenerate lost tokens, the interval after one is transmitted is random for each node.

The other problem is concerned with adding and removing devices from the network. If a device within a sequence is switched off, then apart from losing the token, that device should not be sent any more tokens. It should be removed from the logical ring. If a device that has not been included in the sequence wants to transmit information then it must make another device send it the token. Removing devices is easy, because all that needs to be done is for the preceding device in the sequence to be sent a message to the effect that it should change its destination address for the token to the next-but-one device in the sequence. Adding devices requires the device not in the sequence but wanting to be added to it to broadcast a message asking to be sent the token, together with the address of the next device in the sequence.

The basic token method of access is simple to implement, but allowing for lost tokens, and adding and removing other devices adds considerably to the complexity. Assigning one device as the network controller can simplify matters.

Since the bus topology permits every device to hear all transmissions, it is possible to implement a token-passing scheme in which some devices can be sent information but are never allowed to transmit (B in figure 5.14). This is accomplished by not including them in the token-passing sequence. Because they never get the token they cannot transmit.

The token need not be a separate packet; it can also be a field (usually in the trailer) of a normal information packet. The destination device will read off the information but, of course, all the devices on the network can hear all the packets. The one with the token address will recognise it in the trailer of the information packet and will thus get control.

5.3 PROTOCOL REQUIREMENTS

In Chapter 4 some of the major requirements for data transmission were introduced and the development of data link protocols discussed. Data link protocols are necessary in any real system for handling the transmission of digital data streams reliably over links between devices. Most data link protocols were devised for traditional computer systems employing point-to-point links between terminals and computers, peripherals and their controllers, and latterly for interconnection of computer processors themselves. Some data link protocols have been developed for circuits of the polled multipoint or loop types which are shared by a group of terminal devices under the control of a special piece of equipment.

The common feature of these systems, which helps to simplify the design of data link, and indeed higher-level, protocols, is the knowledge of which device data will come from. In a point-to-point situation the computer, say, at one end of the link knows which terminal is connected to the other end, and hence it is in a position to make assumptions about its characteristics: transmission speed, intelligence, line and page (or screen) format, control characters required, etc. On a polled circuit the controller knows which device is sending data, because the controller itself has given it permission to do so.

Local area networks are designed and operated in a very different manner. One way that this affects the protocol requirement is in the sharing of a common data-transmission resource by a number of independent devices, with no prior agreement being necessary for the exchange of information. Information packets can be transmitted into the network, and heard by all the others in the system, without any knowledge about their characteristics being assumed. The data link layer protocol must take on a different character. For example, both the address of the sender and the destination must be used so that the network (or devices connected to it) can route the messages correctly and, on delivery, the destination device knows from where it came.

A convenient way of treating data communications protocols, with particular relevance to intelligent devices, is the *Reference Model for Open Systems Interconnection*, which has been under development by the International Organization for Standardization (ISO) since 1977. The topic of open systems interconnection is too extensive for this book. The reasons for developing it and the way it can be used are covered in detail in reference [5]. The latest definitive description of the Reference Model is contained in the official paper published by the ISO [6].

The Reference Model (figure 5.15) is the basis for developing a full range of standard protocols for interconnection of computers and computer-related equipment. It consists of a hierarchy of seven layers, each one using those beneath it to provide a service of a particular character, and providing a more complete service to the layers above.

Work on open systems interconnection began when users realised that the full potential of data networks and public packet-switched systems would not be realised if each of the devices on the network demanded its own particular set of protocols as determined by its manufacturer. Traditional computer systems were always *closed*, that is to say the devices conformed to the rules laid down by the manufacturer or designer of the system. All the protocols used by the terminals were determined by the characteristics of the computer or communications controller. Another terminal from another computer manufacturer, or possibly even another range of equipment from the same manufacturer, was unlikely to be usable without first being modified or made to emulate an acceptable model. So long as the number of devices involved was small and all of them were under the strict control of a single group, this situation was acceptable.

However, developments in computing have been such that a great many more computer-related devices are now available that are either designed for, or have their value enhanced by, networking. Such is the variety of devices available now that a closed network is not feasible. Most users and manufacturers now realise that a set of open systems interconnection standards to enable devices to interwork at all levels will be of great benefit. The Reference Model is the first real step towards that goal.

Briefly, the functions of the layers are as follows.

Applications layer The applications layer is the highest layer defined in the Reference Model. It is concerned with directly supporting the exchange of information between end-users, applications programs or devices. Several different types of protocol are needed in this layer: those particular to specific applications and general ones for user and network support (for example, accounting, access control, user verification).

Presentation layer The presentation layer performs the function of

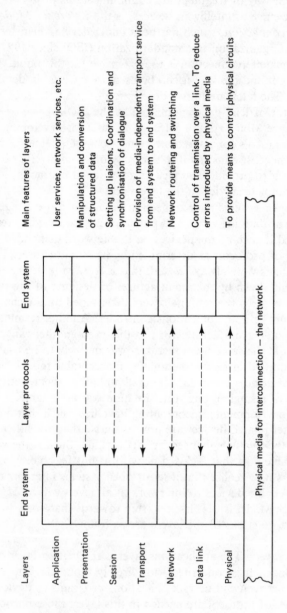

Figure 5.15 Reference model for open systems interconnection

ensuring that data exchanged between devices are presented to the applications or end-user devices in the form that they can understand. This permits different items of equipment using different data formats to converse intelligibly.

Session layer When two applications wish to exchange information in a normal computer system they have to come to some agreement on the form that such an exchange will take. The function of the session layer is to set up this liaison — called a session.

Transport layer The transport layer attempts to provide the layers above it with an ideal or perfect transmission system with the quality of service required. Because the real data transmission network will have various peculiarities, the transport layer endeavours to use the facilities that it has available to mask the undesirable characteristics.

Network layer The network layer performs the normal network functions of switching (circuit or packet) and routeing information between end devices. It can also perform the function of linking two separate networks.

Data link layer Physical data transmission media are notoriously prone to errors in the form of noise, interference, etc. The data link layer enables many of the normal type of transmission errors to be handled and so enhances the quality of service provided.

Physical layer The physical layer provides the means to attach to the physical medium and control its use.

The *physical medium* is not itself part of the reference model although it is important to realise what it contains. In terms of the traditional computer network the physical medium consists of the circuits, public networks, leased lines, etc., and the modems or other line driving equipment necessary to enable the end-user equipment (computers, multiplexers, controllers, terminals, etc.) to connect to them. In a local area network the physical medium would consist of the cables and the repeaters, transceivers or modems, which allow the user equipment to interface to the network.

The Reference Model by itself does not guarantee interconnection. Each of its layers defines a set of functions and services that are implemented in protocols. Some of these protocols are independent of the network in use (such as the upper three layers); others depend on the networks to a greater or lesser extent. The physical layers implemented will be very different for an optical fibre link, for example, as compared with a packet-switched network. The standard data link protocol, high-level data link control (HDLC), is one example of the range of possible protocols for the data link layer. Others may be more valid for some circumstances.

A local area network is just one example of a data-transmission network and it is the intention of most network suppliers that their products be designed around the open system interconnection ideal. The Reference Model was designed before the full potential of local area networks was appreciated and it is more orientated towards traditional computer and packet-switched systems. Figure 5.16 shows an example of the modifications needed to the lowest layers of the Reference Model to meet the requirements of a local area network.

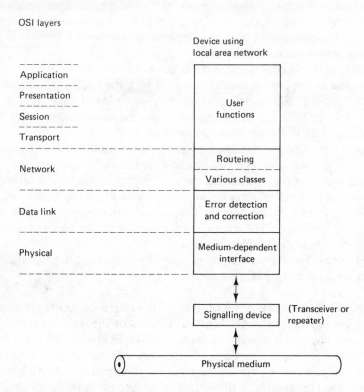

Figure 5.16 Using the OSI reference model for local area networks

The physical layer performs the normal functions of interfacing to the physical media, although in the case of a local area network this depends on the type of repeater, transceiver or modem being used. The data link layer also performs its usual functions of device-to-device error correction, flow control, etc. The 'data link' involved is the shared network, so the type of protocols used will differ from those applicable to point-to-point links or packet-switched systems.

The network layer will handle different classes of service appropriate to different modes of use. For example, some applications demand that an exchange of packets over an extended period must take place in order that sufficient information is transmitted. Others require a single packet or message to perform the data transfer. Many local area networks also provide for broadcast messages to be received by all the users. This class of service would be provided by the network layer. This layer also performs the transfer of data from one network to another, either local or wide area.

Local area networks are primarily concerned with providing a reliable means of data transmission between devices. Thus the data link layer is the main concern of the designers. It was mentioned earlier that on most local area networks the recipient of a packet of information has no prior knowledge of where the next packet will come from. To help resolve the difficulties that this could cause, a high-level data link packet is available — a typical format is shown in figure 5.17. As can be seen both

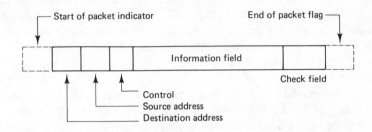

Figure 5.17 Typical packet format for local area network

the source and destination addresses are required. The source address is used by the destination device to find out from where the packet came, and the destination address is used by the network, repeaters, transceivers, etc. to make sure that the packet reaches the appropriate device.

Not all local area network techniques are capable of transmitting a full packet at a time. Typical implementations of the empty slot method for rings can transport only a very limited number of characters at a time. These are passed by the repeater to an intelligent piece of equipment which assembles them into a packet of the form shown in figure 5.17.

The control fields of the packet, or different formats of it, can be used for the different classes of transaction.

In the layers above the data link protocols are the higher-level protocols. One will probably be needed to ensure that more than one program or terminal can use a single access point to the network. Most computer systems in use now operate in a multiprogramming mode in which several programs share the processing power at the same time. More than one of these may be in conversation with another program or terminal elsewhere on the network, but it does not make much sense to provide a large number of network connections for each computer. Thus, a method is needed to differentiate between incoming packets and route them to the appropriate programs. A similar situation exists where several terminals share a single controller which is interfaced to the network.

Above this, the presentation and application layer functions of the open systems interconnection model are also required to handle data format conversion, protocol conversion, authentication, etc.

For these reasons most local area networks provide a set of devices, called the device interface in figure 5.1, in which the particular interface required by the attached device is handled. In general other layers of protocol still have to be provided in the attached device itself, their exact form depending on the application, on the functions provided by the device interface and on the characteristics of the device with which information is being exchanged.

A local area network does not guarantee that the information sent from one device to another will be understandable, it merely tries to ensure that the information will get there. This corresponds to the lowest three levels of the Reference Model for open systems interconnection. It is the responsibility of the user to ensure that the remainder of the reference model is implemented.

It must be realised that local area networks are data-communication systems, and to be of any real use to the end-user they require a wealth of services to be built upon them. Distributed computing, office technology, etc. all require services orientated towards the user.

5.4 ERROR HANDLING

Normal data-transmission networks based on telephone circuits usually exhibit a high error rate when compared with computer systems. Networks designed specifically for digital data transmission are generally much better in this respect. Local area networks are generally designed to give very low error rates.

When employing normal data-transmission circuits the user must build special error-detecting and correcting procedures into the data communications procedures. The high-level data link control (HDLC) data link protocol is designed to provide a sophisticated level of service in this respect. The responsibility for handling errors is left to the equipment using the network rather than the network itself.

Well-designed local area networks seldom pass undetected errors to the equipment connected to them for two reasons. The first is because the network itself is designed to transport digital information over short distances. It is much easier to ensure error-free transmissions when the distance covered is small and the quality of the equipment and media involved is easily controlled. The second reason for low error rates is that various error-detecting procedures are employed in the network itself, both to detect transient transmission errors and to detect portions of the networks that are deteriorating in quality.

Network 'errors' can occur in two forms: (a) transmission faults, which corrupt the data being transported by the network, and (b) network operation faults, which affect the operation of the network as a whole. The latter group is concerned with items such as packets continuing to circulate around a ring without being removed. Monitoring the network operations, or providing monitoring and correction schemes in the access mechanism, can be used to handle faults of this character. This subject is better left until the chapter on performance (Chapter 7) in which the subject of monitoring is treated in detail.

This section is concerned with the detection and correction of errors belonging to the first category: transmission faults.

We have already shown that the transmission channels on a local area network can be used in two fundamentally different ways. Firstly, the channel capacity can be divided up in such a way that no two devices will be able to transmit at the same instant. Secondly, devices contend with each other directly for the channel and rely on the occurrence of errors to detect when more than one is transmitting simultaneously. The first situation is found in most ring-based systems, or in techniques that ensure that the control of the network is passed sequentially from one device to another. The second situation is typical of contention-broadcast networks.

In networks in which contention cannot occur there is no possibility of a packet of data being corrupted by another device. The only errors likely to occur are due to noise and interference. The standard computer technique of parity checking is quite sufficient for many cases where the network is generally error free and the quantity of data transmitted at a time is small. To illustrate how parity checking works in practice the operation of an empty slot ring will be considered.

Because an empty slot ring usually employs a short packet size for carrying data around the ring, the packet being transported in short hops from one repeater to the next, the use of parity is ideal for this sort of situation. With longer packets the possibility of the occurrence of two errors is more likely and a simple parity check would miss them. Each packet is read into the repeater and is retransmitted bit by bit with the minimum of delay. The whole packet is not stored within the repeater at any time, the first bit being retransmitted as soon as possible and before much of the rest of the packet has been received. The repeater keeps track of the parity of the data stream that it has received and, rather than just retransmitting the last bit (that is, the parity bit), it transmits the parity bit that it has calculated itself. It then checks the parity bit on the incoming packet to see if the two match. If they do not, then there must have been an error in the packet when it was received and this can be reported. Generally, the next empty packet that it receives is used to report the error to a monitoring device; the latter can analyse the occurrence of errors and can tell if one part of the network is deteriorating. This can be reported to a human supervisor so that corrective action can be taken.

Naturally, the ultimate destination may not know that the packet of data received is in error, since the parity may have been reset by an earlier repeater. Since the network packets are generally too short to be used for transporting a usefully sized message in empty slot rings, a higher-level data link protocol is employed with more sophisticated error-checking procedures which will detect most errors in a long message or frame. These are very similar to the techniques employed in contention systems, or where long packets are transported by the network. These will be considered next.

HDLC employs a field (the frame check sequence) following the information to check the contents of the whole frame for errors. The technique used employs *polynominal codes*, an explanation of which is beyond the scope of this book. Reference [7] presents an explanation of how polynominal codes work, and reference [8] explains how they are used for data transmission. Since this method has proved very effective in detecting errors, it is employed as the standard technique for most local area networks.

Contention broadcast networks rely on the detection of errors to determine when more than one device has transmitted at the same time. The complexity of the checking procedure may be greater than that used in HDLC in order to ensure with more certainty the detection of contention on the network.

5.5 STANDARDS ACTIVITIES

A local area network consists of more than just a network of cables along which information travels from one device to another. A signalling device or transmitter is needed by every device using the network, as well as a receiver for the incoming transmissions. In addition, a method of accessing and using the network in a controlled manner has to be laid down, otherwise the situation on the cables would quickly degenerate into chaos. For these reasons, as soon as it was realised that local area networks were going to be produced and sold in quantity, work began on standardising various aspects of the networks. Early and appropriate standards will make it simpler for the user to obtain interfaces or other pieces of equipment that will work properly on the network and that can be guaranteed to exchange information at the correct speed and in the right format with others on the network.

Standards for local area networks can be produced for the signalling method (that is, baseband or broadband, Manchester encoding or another technique, the access method (CSMA/CD, empty slot, etc.), the transmission speed, the packet format, the network addressing convention, the cable itself and ways of attaching to it.

The Xerox Corporation in the USA was one of the first to apply itself to local area networking standards by actively promoting its Ethernet system. To help Ethernet to become accepted as an industry standard by as many potential customers as possible, Xerox set up an Ethernet consortium with the Intel Corporation (manufacturers of large-scale integrated electronics) and Digital Equipment Corporation (manufacturers of minicomputer systems). During 1980 this consortium produced its specification for Ethernet [9]. Since then, Ethernet has been very strongly promoted as the standard for a baseband-bus local area network.

The Institute of Electrical and Electronic Engineers (IEEE) in the USA also decided to examine the possibilities for standardisation of local area networks. It found that among its members there was significant opposition to the adoption of Ethernet as the one and only local area network standard for a number of reasons. Ethernet is suitable only for bus networks and there is sufficient demand for ring systems to warrant a standard for these as well as for buses. Also, certain industrial and process control applications demand a level of reliability and guaranteed access which is difficult to achieve with Ethernet in its standard form.

IEEE decided to examine the possibilities for standardising an Ethernet type of system, to meet the demands for a straightforward baseband-bus system, and simultaneously a token-passing technique. The token-passing technique can be implemented on rings or bus networks and can have a level of priority built into it to meet the requirements of real-time process control users. Their aims are published in reference [10].

The empty slot ring technique, of which the Cambridge ring is the best known example, is strongly supported by users in the UK, especially by the universities. An industry standard empty slot ring is being proposed, designed to operate at speeds around 50 Mbps. The proponents see this standard as coexisting with the IEEE standards and Ethernet. It is likely that the work will be progressed by the British Standards Institution, with most of the user effort coming from the academic community, with the support of interested suppliers. The empty slot proposals could also be actively presented to the IEEE.

REFERENCES

1 Davies, D. W., Barber, D. L. A., Price, W. L. and Solomonides, C. M., *Computer Networks and their Protocols*, John Wiley, Chichester, 1979.

2 Clark, D. D., Pogran, K. T. and Reed, D. P., 'An Introduction to Local Area Networks', *Proceedings of the IEEE*, Volume 66 No. 11 (November 1978) 1497–1517.

3 Penney, B. K. and Baghdadi, A. A., 'Survey of Computer Communications Loop Networks: Parts 1 and 2', *Computer Communications*, Volume 2 No. 4 (August 1979) 165–180; Volume 2 No. 5 (October 1979) 224–241.

4 Kleinrock, L., *Queueing Systems. Volume II Computer Applications*, John Wiley, Chichester, 1979.

5 Gee, K. C. E., *An Introduction to Open System Interconnection*, NCC Publications, Manchester, 1980.

6 International Organization for Standardization, *Reference Model for Open Systems Interconnection*, DIS 7498, ISO, Geneva (documents obtainable from National Standards bodies — British Standards Institution, London, in the UK).

7 Pritchard, J. A. T., *Quantitative Methods in On-Line Systems*, NCC Publications, Manchester, 1977.

8 Cole, R., *Computer Communications*, Macmillan, London, 1982, chapter 6.

9 Digital Equipment Corporation, Intel Corporation and Xerox Corporation, *The Ethernet: A Local Area Network Data Link Layer and Physical Layer Specification*, DEC, Intel and Xerox, September 1980 (obtainable from Xerox Corporation, OPD Systems Development, 3450 Hillview Avenue, Palo Alto, CA 94304, USA).

10 IEEE Computer Society Local Area Networks Standards Committee, *Functional Requirements Document*, Version 5.2, IEEE, New York, February 1981.

6 *Examples of Local Area Networks*

In previous chapters the basic techniques used in constructing local area networks have been examined. In this chapter some of the ways in which these techniques have been put together will be presented. By no means all the possible combinations of access method, topology, medium, etc. have been exhausted. Some of them are difficult to implement, too expensive or just not sensible.

Local area networks have been a product of research establishments, of which four are probably the most significant in terms of the influence that they had on subsequent development: Xerox's Palo Alto Research Center, University of Cambridge, Mitre Corporation and Hasler. The systems chosen for discussion here are representative of the main techniques in use today.

The chapter concludes with a brief examination of other promising options.

6.1 ETHERNET

Ethernet is both a product and a technique. The product is a local area networking system marketed by the Xerox Corporation (Rank Xerox in the UK) as the basic communications network for their range of electronic office systems products. The technique used for data transmission in this network is licensed by the Xerox, Digital Equipment and Intel Corporations and forms the underlying philosphy of several other local area network products: complete networks, complete systems (networks, processors, services and devices) and individual devices.

The aim of this licensing procedure is to ensure that a wide range of equipment will be usable on any network that uses the Ethernet technique as defined by Xerox *et al*. This includes not only the standard access method, but also a naming and addressing scheme, such that every device worldwide made for an Ethernet system will have a unique identifier.

6.1.1 Ethernet — Palo Alto Research Center

The Xerox Corporation in the USA designed Ethernet as an experimental system for use within their Palo Alto Research Center establishment during the early 1970s. Its purpose was to connect office workstations to expensive computers, file storage devices and other items of office equipment, so that these expensive devices could be shared by a large population of users of relatively low-cost equipment.

The cheapness of the majority of the devices using the network was a very significant influence on the design of Ethernet. The communications system had to be cheap compared with the attached devices (excluding the expensive shared items), the justification of this being that no one would be interested in buying a network if it cost more to connect to it than the devices themselves. The rapidly falling cost of computing equipment, especially the personal computers, intelligent terminals and office workstations intended for Ethernet, severely restricted the choice of network, and effectively excluded the standard technique of using separate cables, multiplexers, line drivers or modems and controllers.

Apart from the cost, a number of other factors were considered to be important to the designers of Ethernet

- the network as a whole had to be very reliable, and the failure of any single component (except possibly the cable) should not affect the operation of the rest;
- the running costs, including necessary overheads and the maintenance, should be low;
- there should be no central controller, and thus the access control should be distributed around the network;
- since the bulk of the devices envisaged for use on Ethernet would be based on computer technology, the network should be particularly suitable for handling traffic that comes in bursts;
- the network, and its interface devices, must be unobtrusive in a normal office environment.

One result of meeting these requirements was to make the network as simple in concept and operation as possible. It was felt that conventional polling techniques and fixed-slot, time-division multiplexing would be unsuitable since, apart from being more expensive and complex, they were not well suited to handling data that are transmitted in bursts.

The medium chosen for transmission was coaxial cable since it was easy to obtain and was inherently capable of transporting data at high speeds over relatively long distances without the need for special shielding or repeaters. It was also decided to adopt the bus topology and use a broadcast method developed from radio broadcast experiments carried out by the University of Hawaii for its ALOHA network. Ethernet topology is in the form of a tree structure, with discrete ends to the buses, and no loops.

The contention system of sharing the bus was used because it looked well suited to handling traffic in bursts. The key to understanding the Ethernet concept is neither the medium used nor the topology of the network; it lies in the way that each attached device gains access to the network and shares the transmission capacity with others. Information to be transmitted is placed in a packet held in a buffer, together with the addresses of the sender and destination and a complex error-check field. When the network is quiet, the packet is transmitted, during which time the sending device also listens to the broadcast to check that it sounds the same as it is in the buffer. The system is easy to understand provided that no one else transmits at the same time. It is to meet this problem of possible collisions that Ethernet contains some special design features developed at Palo Alto.

If another device also decides to transmit at the same instant, the resulting signal heard on the cable will differ from both of the two packets being broadcast; the sender (and any listeners, because the error-check fields will reveal that rubbish has been received) will then realise that the packets have collided with one another. The Ethernet rules say that each sender then ceases transmission and retries a random time interval later. The details of the technique, now usually called *carrier sense multiple access with collision detection (CSMA/CD)* have been explained in Chapter 5. In earlier contention systems the sender did not listen to the broadcast and so could waste time transmitting information that was intermingled with other packets from other users.

The method has proved very successful in practice in minimising the channel time wasted owing to simultaneous transmission, although it is suited mainly to short-distance networks. It is especially good for systems that use only a small portion of the total network traffic capacity and whose individual devices transmit information in short bursts. Long periods of continuous transmission from one device can upset the pattern of use of the complete network. The technique is also reasonably easy to implement in terms of the design of the network interface hardware and access software.

Ethernet, and the CSMA/CD access method, are probably the most important techniques currently being used for local area networks. Not only can they be implemented as a single bus network (standard Ethernet) but CSMA/CD can be incorporated into other network designs, as will be mentioned briefly in the next section.

6.1.2 Commercial Ethernet

Following successful trials at Palo Alto and elsewhere, during the 1970s Xerox upgraded the network specification and, in 1980 published, together with DEC and Intel, their definition of Ethernet [1].

This version retains the form of the carrier sense multiple access with collision detection (CSMA/CD) technique developed in the Palo Alto Research Center. A summary of Ethernet's major characteristics follows.

Topology   Tree-shaped composed of separate bus segments. No more than two repeaters (devices that regenerate signals and link segments) are permitted between any two devices. This slightly restricts the network topology, with the best solution being one where a 'backbone' bus is used to which all the other bus segments are connected (figure 3.14).
Medium   Coaxial cable of 50 ohm impedance. Each segment must have 50 ohm terminators at each end. To assist in connecting to the cable it should have markings every 2.5 metres since certain types of connector can upset the electrical properties unless placed at multiples of this spacing.
Signalling system   Baseband, bit-serial, Manchester encoded.
Data transmission rate   10 Mbps.
Maximum station separation   2.5 km.
Maximum length of cable segment   500 metres.
Maximum number of stations per network   1024.
Access method   Normal CSMA/CD.
Frame   A variable length frame (72 to 1526 bytes) with the format shown in figure 6.1. A special preamble field indicates the start of the frame. There is no end-of-frame marker.
Addressing   Both the source and destination addresses are included in the frame, and each is 48 bits long. The first bit of the destination field is a *multicast* bit which is switched on whenever every device in a 'block' (to be defined next) is to receive the message. The next 23-bit field is the block number and is allocated to the licence holder. The next 24 bits represent the number of the device within that block, and are allocated by the holder of that block number. The source address field always has the first bit set to 0.

Although the data-transmission rate is 10 Mbps the network is shared by every user of the system, so the actual data transfer rate between any two devices will always be much less in practice. A high raw data-transmission rate is essential in this type of system to ensure that each pair of devices in conversation can obtain an adequate transfer rate without having to wait too long. The addressing scheme is intended to ensure that each device made for Ethernet is unique so that separate Ethernet systems can be linked (by wide area networks for example) and the same address as a local user can be used.

Field lengths (bytes)

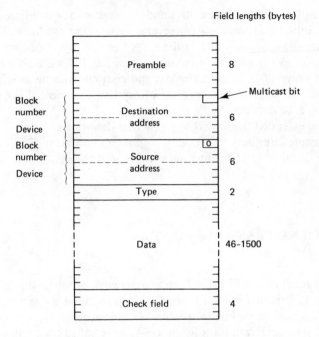

Figure 6.1 Ethernet frame format

Transceivers are used to permit end-user devices to be connected to an Ethernet system. The transceiver merely provides the signalling and listening circuits for the other devices. Data to be transmitted must first be placed in a packet of the correct type with the correct address, etc. The attached device must also decide when to send, detect when a packet collides with another, etc.

In actual working networks, Ethernet has been demonstrated to perform well. Special simulations of highly loaded networks have been made to test the adequacy of the technique and efficiencies of around 97 per cent have been achieved under these conditions. One possible area of concern relates to the way a packet is delayed on a very busy network. Under Ethernet rules, the station attempting to transmit a packet that is corrupted by a collision with another must wait for a length of time before trying to send it again. If it again does not succeed it has to wait for a longer period. This means that a station that is unsuccessful is slowed down by other transmissions, even though it may be their first attempt. However, the combination of high transmission rate, the fairly low use of available capacity normally experienced, and the tendency for digital data devices to transmit in short bursts with longer gaps between, means that this situation rarely occurs. Ethernet has proved to perform well in practice.

Because of its proven capabilities and the ease with which licences can be obtained, Ethernet is the basis for several networking products. The Ungermann–Bass organisation in the USA has developed a network that uses Ethernet as the basic transmission technique, but with devices provided to allow a range of ordinary terminals and computers to be interfaced to it. The system, called Net/One, was one of the first commercial Ethernet-based local area networks to be marketed.

Net/One extended the underlying Ethernet data-transmission network to provide simple interfaces to ordinary computer equipment. The same technique could be used for any networking technology.

6.2 OTHER BASEBAND BUS SYSTEMS

HYPERchannel and HYPERbus are two network products that use similar techniques to Ethernet but with modifications to avoid the increasing delays caused when packets collide in transit. The designers of the system, the Network Systems Corporation in the USA, have called their technique *carrier sense multiple access with collision avoidance (CSMA/CA)*.

CSMA/CA works in the following manner. If the network has been quiet for some time then a station with data to send first listens to make sure no other device is transmitting and if not it transmits. If no collisions occur, the destination device sends back an acknowledgement packet. This happens immediately and is hardware controlled. The acknowledgement itself cannot collide because after each transmission the network enters a different mode in which stations cannot transmit whenever they like but only within preallocated time slots. During this mode each station is given the opportunity to transmit in their time slot without any possibility of a collision occurring. If all the time slots are unused the network then enters the 'free-for-all' state in which devices can transmit when they want to. If a collision occurs during the free-for-all state no acknowledgement is sent, so the sender then uses its preallocated time slot to send the packet again.

The technique is essentially a combination of a contention-based method and a standard time-division multiplexed system. It is designed for networks with a small number of stations or access points. With a large number of devices sending information at regular intervals the network could spend an excessively long time in the 'preallocated time slot' phase, in which most of the slots will remain unused.

HYPERchannel was the first commercial network to use this technique. It is designed primarily for interconnecting a limited number of high-speed devices, such as mainframe computers, their peripherals and device controllers. The data-transmission rate of HYPERchannel is 50 Mbps for each cable, and up to four cables can be run in parallel giving a possible 200 Mbps transmission rate on the network. Each cable is treated as a separate network by the interface units. HYPERchannel is generally used only to interconnect mainfràme computers and a few terminals.

HYPERbus is aimed at the market for interconnecting large numbers of lower-speed devices using the normal local area network approach. It operates at 6.312 Mbps raw transmission rate using an adaptation of the CSMA/CA scheme. It seems to be ideal as a feeder network for connection into a HYPERchannel system to allow ultimate access to mainframe systems. Although HYPERbus is a contention-bus system normally using coaxial cable, provision has been made in the design for using optical fibres. In this case two cables are used to permit information to flow in both directions from the interface devices.

6.3 CAMBRIDGE RING

6.3.1 University of Cambridge Computer Laboratory

During the early 1970s the Computer Laboratory of the University of Cambridge was engaged in experiments with distributed computing. It soon became obvious that a method of interconnecting computers, their terminals, and other similar devices within a building or restricted site was needed. In order to provide the bandwidth needed for moving quantities of data from one computer to another, while transferring files for example, the communications system had to be capable of operating at a data-transmission rate considerably greater than those provided by normal tele-communications circuits.

The original design of the Cambridge ring, begun in 1974, was modelled closely on the Hasler ring then operating at Hasler's Berne Research Laboratories (see later). The Cambridge people thought that a ring network would be eminently suitable for the distributed computing tasks since it is simple in concept and appeared to be easy to implement in practice. The register insertion technique that had been adopted by Hasler offered the ability to share the transmission capacity of the ring fairly among all the attached devices. In addition the technique also offered a method of confirming the successful or otherwise delivery of each packet transported. This is an important requirement for any network built to carry computer data.

During early experiments the Cambridge team realised that certain problems existed with the register insertion technique. Namely, if a register in any station or repeater on the ring develops a fault the operation of the whole of the rest of the ring is disrupted. If that fault is in a station that is not currently involved in a data exchange, then the fault does not become apparent until that station attempts transmission, at which point it is too late to prevent it. Since the Cambridge team also had considerable doubt at that time concerning their ability to make reliable register insertion devices that could operate at the speeds desired, they opted for another technique based on a continuously circulating packet — the *empty slot* method. The register insertion devices already built were easily modified since much of the circuitry for the two methods is similar.

The most important result of the Cambridge Computer Laboratory work was to establish that the empty slot technique (now known as the Cambridge ring) worked well and was easy to implement. They also soon realised the need for a special-purpose device on the network to remove slots that are filled but not emptied by the sender for various reasons. The ring installed at the Computer Laboratory in Cambridge uses, for most of its length, two pairs of ordinary twisted-pair cable operating in a baseband mode at a data-transmission rate round the ring of 10 Mbps. The slot used is very small when compared with typical message sizes (figure 6.2). It is 38 bits in length and its fields are as follows

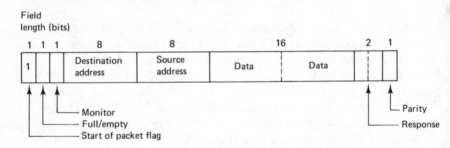

Figure 6.2 Basic Cambridge ring slot format

Bit	Function
1	Flag bit to indicate the beginning of the slot.
2	Full/empty bit.
3	Monitor bit.

Bits 2 and 3 are used together:

11	Indicates that the sender has just transmitted the slot.
10	Set by the monitor station to indicate that the slot has passed it once. If the monitor receives a slot with this set it knows that the sender has not 'emptied' it — hence error.
00	Set by the sender to empty the slot.
01	Set by the monitor in an empty slot. If the slot returns with 01 still set the rest of the slot is checked for errors.

4–11 Destination address. Address 0 is the monitor. Address 255 is a
broadcast address applicable to every device.

12–19 Source address.

20–35 Data fields.

36–37 Response field, used as follows:

    11 Set by the sender. If still set on return the slot has been ignored.

    10 Set by the recipient to indicate that the slot was rejected.

    01 Set by the recipient if slot accepted.

    00 Set by the recipient to indicate that it was busy and unable to process the slot.

38 Parity bit. Reset by each repeater as the slot passes through it.

The repeaters used operate very rapidly so that slots are not delayed while being processed. Figure 6.3 shows the schematic construction of a ring interface. The repeater provides the station with the contents of the slot and allows the slot to be modified. The access box performs the function of converting the ring protocols into the protocols and interface that the attached device requires.

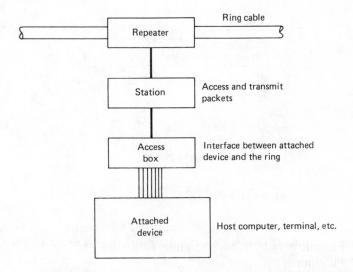

Figure 6.3 Cambridge ring interface

Two pairs of twisted-pair cable are used to transmit the data in the following way: a change in state on both pairs simultaneously indicates bit 1; on one pair only indicates bit 0. Since it is necessary for both pairs to be sensed together small differences in lengths between the individual conductors and between the pairs can upset the signalling. For this reason the repeaters are normally placed close together, generally not more than 100 metres apart.

The repeaters themselves are generally powered directly from the ring cable by means of power supplies which inject a direct current into the ring at various locations. In this way the attached devices can be switched off or removed leaving the repeater still able to function properly. The ring is also often provided with jack plugs so that repeaters can be inserted without the cable having to be cut. While the repeater is actually being plugged in some slots in transit will be corrupted, but normal error-detection procedures will generally eliminate errors before they reach the end user.

In the Computer Laboratory at Cambridge there is a section of optical fibre. This can be installed easily in a Cambridge ring and using this medium the distances between repeaters can be much greater than for twisted pair cables.

Because the slot size on a Cambridge ring is so limited it is usual to provide higher-level protocols to handle normal size packets and messages more easily. The *basic block protocol* is the one that is used as an HDLC type of data link protocol. The format of a basic block is shown in figure 6.4. The field labelled port number is used to enable separate application

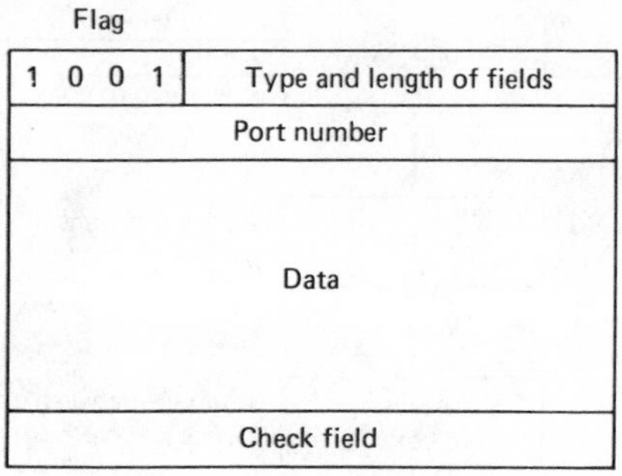

Flag

1 0 0 1	Type and length of fields
Port number	
Data	
Check field	

Figure 6.4 Basic block format

programs in a host or separate devices attached to a controller to be addressed individually through a single ring interface. The data field itself is variable in length.

The basic block protocol is used to transmit single blocks of information between end-users. Each basic block is itself transmitted, 16 bits at a time, in the data fields of the ring slot shown in figure 6.2. Various ways of using this basic block protocol have been devised to meet specific applications.

One common requirement for data-transmission systems is the trans-action/response form of exchange. The transaction may consist of a short message (a line of input from a terminal for example), and an immediate response is needed. A protocol called the *single shot protocol* has been designed to meet this requirement. It uses the basic block protocol with the header field set to a special bit pattern to identify this mode of use. Various parameters can be set to indicate the function of the transaction. The response block uses return codes and parameters to indicate success or failure.

Another requirement of distributed computing networks is to be able to move long streams of data (a file or record for example) from one location to another. The *byte stream protocol* has been designed to meet these requirements. It uses the basic block protocol to ensure error-free data transmission.

Most of the products that have been developed from the Cambridge ring have implemented these protocols.

6.3.2 Near-standard Cambridge Rings

Although the original Cambridge ring used a ring slot size of 3 bits, this is not very convenient for implementing some higher-level protocols. Most implementations have decided to use longer slots, the easiest to implement being one of 40 bits, with two extra bits after the data field.

It is then easy to set a switch in the repeater and access box to indicate whether 38 or 40 bit slots are in use. Some examples of typical commercial systems are

Logica VTS — Polynet   38 or 40 bit slots, repeaters operate at a lower voltage than the Cambridge installation.
Orbis Computers/Acorn Computers   Standard Cambridge system.
Toltec Computer Ltd — DataRing   40 bit slots, adaptable to 38 bit.
Scientific and Electronic Enterprises Ltd — Transring   38 bit slots.

6.3.3 PLANET

PLANET is an empty slot ring that is slightly different from the normal type of Cambridge ring considered earlier. It is designed and marketed by Racal–Milgo.

PLANET (Private Local Area Network) uses a coaxial cable transmission medium which is duplicated for back-up purposes. Consequently the baseband signalling technique employed differs considerably from the normal Cambridge ring.

For reliability, the access points on the network are passive and require no power, unlike the repeaters normally employed. A network monitoring device is required, called in this case the administrator.

The slot size is 42 bits, in which 16 bits are used for data. The format is shown in figure 6.5.

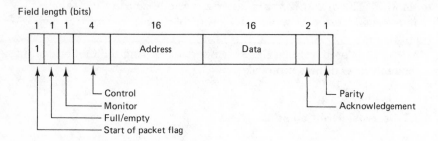

Figure 6.5 PLANET's ring packet format

When compared with the Cambridge ring's slot it can be seen that four extra control bits are used preceding the address fields. This control field is used to indicate the way the address and data fields are used in this particular slot.

It is possible to set up higher-level services different from those normally supplied with Cambridge rings. Apart from the usual broadcast slot facility (in which a single slot or message is addressed to a group or all of the other users on the ring) four other types have been devised all of which involved the establishment of a 'call', or liaison between two devices

1 *Fixed calls*   The administrator is told that two ring users require to be in permanent contact, so it establishes a permanent liaison (permanent virtual circuit) between them.
2 *Designated calls*   Designated calls are fixed calls set up by a ring user, rather than the administrator, using a specially designated access point. The calls set up will be for other users on the network.
3 *Switched calls*   Switched calls exist only for the duration of the message exchange.
4 *Diagnostic calls*   Diagnostic calls occur between the administrator and the access devices (the so-called terminal access points) rather than the attached devices themselves. As the name suggests they are used to check the operation of the network.

6.4 BROADBAND SYSTEMS

Broadband networks are much more suitable for some applications than baseband systems. In particular, broadband transmissions are much less susceptible to interference from electrical machinery. It was just this feature that was used to advantage by early broadband networks that were designed for industrial process control.

Broadband networks can, however, be used for many other purposes and can give the user a much wider bandwidth, and consequently total throughput, than practically every other viable system. The wide bandwidth makes them especially suitable for very demanding applications such as real-time colour television. The ability of broadband systems to handle analogue and digital information equally easily is also of value for networks intended to be used for integrated communications systems, such as computer-generated data and ordinary telephone conversations (in their analogue form).

The Mitre Corporation provided much of the experimental work on contention broadband networks with their two MITRIX systems, and latterly with MITRENET. The techniques have been further developed into marketable products by several suppliers, notably Sytek and Wang.

6.4.1 The Mitre Corporation

The Mitre Corporation in the USA approached the problem of short-distance networking in a manner different from Xerox's Ethernet. Mitre were faced with serving a growing number of their terminal users who wanted to be able to access more than one host computer system, providing data processing, word processing, electronic mail, software development facilities, etc. The normal solution would have been to install a separate terminal for each host computer to be accessed, with a dedicated line between it and the computer system involved. However, the thought of installing separate star-shaped networks for all their computers was rather daunting, to say nothing of being excessively costly. Mitre decided to adapt the techniques of the cable television industry to data transmission.

In the USA it is common to use cable television services rather than individual aerials for every home, as is the case in the UK. The cable used is basically fairly ordinary coaxial cable, but with a usable frequency bandwidth of 300–400 MHz. Since the system is designed for long life and continuous operation in all conditions, and was intended to cover areas the size of a town, the equipment available off-the-shelf seemed suitable for use in a local computer network.

A major problem facing the user of cable television techniques for data transmission is the limited number of standard television channels that can be accommodated within the 300–400 MHz bandwidth. Since a television channel occupies 6 MHz, which is much more than is needed for most data-transmission purposes, the number of point-to-point, two-way links could prove too few in a population serving hundreds of users. More significant, however, is the fact that each channel is equivalent to a dedicated point-to-point wire circuit and it is difficult for a sender to switch from one destination device to another. Mitre decided that both these problems could be successfully overcome by applying time-division multiplexing techniques to individual channels.

Their first major step was the MITRIX system. This used a simple time-division technique in which time slots were assigned to each user within a channel. The system worked well for users who transmitted data fairly continuously, but in general it made poor use of the total capacity of the system.

The network was subsequently developed into a dual-mode system in which high-usage devices were assigned dedicated unique time slots, but low-speed or bursty devices shared a common set. The implementation was naturally more complex as the devices sharing time slots had to examine their slots before using them in case other users were transmitting. If collisions occurred, then back-off and retry procedures had to be followed.

The next development made by Mitre was during the late 1970s with MITRENET. In MITRENET the CSMA/CD technique developed for Ethernet was applied to channels allocated by frequency division in a network based on cable television technology. This system has proved to be very successful in most respects. Very high usage devices requiring continuous channel capacity for long periods can be allocated separate frequency channels which are not shared and thus look like private leased telephone circuits. In fact analogue transmission (voice, television, etc.) can use the same cable, since these services can also be given dedicated bands in the total frequency bandwidth.

6.4.2 Videodata

The Videodata system was developed by the Interactive Systems organisation in the USA (marketed by the 3M Company in the UK) to serve individual requirements for a highly reliable shared-cable system that could operate in electrically noisy environments. The particular characteristics of modulated carrier waves and coaxial cables provide this sort of service.

The current Videodata system is very flexible and can offer three different classes of service

1 *Point-to-point* This is the simplest form of channel that can be provided on a frequency-division multiplexed system. The pairs of devices involved each use a pair of frequencies, one for each direction of transmission, and a pair of complementary fixed-frequency modems. It is useful for permanent connections between pairs of devices and is cheap and simple to implement.

2 *Multidrop* The multidrop configuration involves several devices sharing a single frequency channel in a manner analogous to an ordinary multipoint circuit. A controller is required to poll the individual devices. This function is provided by a headend device.

3 *Distributed communications* The last option uses a special polling channel through which the headend device controls a number of other devices. When these are ready to send or be involved in data exchange the headend assigns to them, and to the other devices involved, another frequency channel. They then use this independently from other users. To make this system work each attached device must use a frequency-agile modem capable of switching between all the possible channels. This is an example of circuit-switching on a frequency-division multiplexed system.

Videodata uses the frequencies within the band 5–108 MHz for the forward channels, and 170–300 MHz for the reverse direction.

6.4.3 WangNet

Wang Laboratories have developed Mitre's MITRENET ideas in a straightforward manner by adopting a two-cable system. Using a two-cable system the full frequency bandwidth of around 300 or 400 MHz can be used for each direction of transmission, giving a total usable bandwidth of 600–800 MHz. In WangNet 340 MHz is used. This is divided into three separate bands

1 *WANGBAND* WANGBAND is for communications between Wang's own processors and equipment and operates in a shared mode using a form of CSMA/CD access method. The total data transmission rate is 12 Mbps.

2 *INTERCONNECT BAND* This band is used to interconnect devices from other suppliers and terminals. It can use dedicated 64 Kbps channels, multipoint (polled) or point-to-point channels at 9.6 Kbps, and a number of circuit-switched channels. The last option requires frequency-agile modems controlled by a special controller on the network.

3 *UTILITY BAND*   This band is intended to be split into separate channels for information not generated by computer, for example: analogue or digital voice, television, videoconferencing, etc.

6.4.4 LocalNet

LocalNet is a further development of the MITRENET techniques using a single coaxial cable. Sytek, part of the Network Resources Corporation organisation in the USA, developed the network and Network Technology Ltd in the UK market it.

The total frequency bandwidth of the single cable is divided into two bands. Allocated so far are 40–106 MHz for transmission, and 196–262 MHz for reception. To make this work the headend device listens to the whole of the transmit band and retransmits all the information on a frequency 156 MHz greater. The modems all listen to the channels within the higher band and transmit in the lower band. Not all the available bandwidth has been utilised and it is known that a circuit-switching class of service is going to be introduced in the future.

At present two forms of LocalNet are available

1 *LocalNet System 20*   This is a relatively low-speed system. It uses channels in the 70–106 MHz band for transmitting and 226–262 MHz for receiving. 120 channels are available, each of 300 KHz bandwidth and 128 Kbps data-transmission rate; each is shared on the contention-bus principle using a form of the CSMA/CD access method.
2 *LocalNet System 40*   By using 6 MHz channels and running these at 2 Mbps each, a higher-speed version of the system is possible. System 40 uses channels in the 40–70 MHz band for transmission and 196–226 MHz for receiving. CSMA/CD is also used to share the capacity of each channel among devices.

The two versions use different frequency bands so that they can be run side by side on the same cable and are completely compatible. Special bridging devices are available to enable a device using one channel to communicate with another device on another channel. These operate by retransmitting the information at a different frequency and by altering the speed if one channel uses System 20 and the other System 40.

Attachment of all user devices to the network is through intelligent interface units which incorporate the radio-frequency modems, the access method logic, the device interface, protocol conversions and data encryption, if necessary.

6.5 MICROCOMPUTER-BASED NETWORKS

A major feature of local area networks is their suitability, from the cost and high degree of interconnection points of view, for linking large numbers of microcomputers or microprocessor-based personal workstations. Microprocessor devices are usually cheap since they are made in large quantities, but personal computers and workstations frequently need to access other devices which are much more expensive. The most obvious examples are magnetic disk storage units (floppy disks or hard high-capacity units) and printers.

Floppy disk units are themselves relatively cheap but when two, say, are provided for every workstation or microcomputer in an office, then the total cost can be very high. Add to this the need to provide maintenance for all these devices which, having electromechanical components, will most definitely be needed at fairly frequent intervals if they are in constant use, and the cost will be too great for many organisations.

It makes much more sense to provide a highly reliable high-capacity hard disk unit which can be shared by all the users on the network, with a bare minimum of floppy disk units being needed to load new software, move data to other devices not on the network, provide security back-ups, etc. The provision of printers for sharing is also required, especially if the microcomputers require occasional hard-copy output.

The cost of the individual devices on the network is generally so low that a network necessary to link them all to these shared devices should also be fairly cheap, when considered on the basis of cost per device. Local area networks can provide this level of cheap interconnection, provided that the access methods and network signalling procedures used are reasonably simple and do not need complex logic to implement. Since the input and output requirements of microcomputer-based devices are relatively slow compared with minicomputers and mainframes, the data-transmission speed of a local network designed explicitly for them need not be very high. This makes it easier to provide interfaces that are cheap.

A number of networks have been provided that meet the requirements. In most instances the suppliers of the networks are also the suppliers of the microcomputers themselves. It is always much simpler to provide a network that is designed to handle only one type of device. Brief descriptions of two typical examples of microcomputer local area networks follow, both employing contention-bus interconnection, based on CSMA/CD, but adapted in various ways to suit the particular requirements of the devices that they are made to interconnect.

6.5.1 Cluster/One (Nestar)

The Cluster/One local area network in its 'Model A' form is intended to interconnect Apple personal computers. It was designed by Nestar in the USA and is supplied by Zynar in the UK. An earlier version of Cluster/One was able to connect several popular makes of microcomputer, but it was decided that adequate facilities at less cost could be provided by standardising on Apple microcomputers.

A typical Cluster/One network is shown in figure 6.6. The file server has a hard disk unit which serves all the Apple microcomputers. The file server itself is another Apple which incorporates some special hardware and software. When each of the other Apples is switched on the file server loads it with the operating system and allocates any file work areas requested. In effect each Apple workstation then performs as would a normal Apple microcomputer using normal floppy disk drives.

The print servers on the network allow various types of printer to be shared by everyone. These servers are also Apple microcomputers configured in special ways to suit their particular requirements.

The network uses a form of CSMA/CD based on multicore cable; either 16-way flat ribbon or round multicore. Using multiway cable has a number of advantages. More than one conductor can be used to carry data in parallel, thus allowing the signalling rate on each to be significantly lower than would be needed to achieve the same transmission speed serially. Other conductors can be used for clocking and to indicate that the network is 'in use'. This last mentioned conductor is especially useful in simplifying the carrier sensing of the network. A device with data ready to send will first check that this conductor is switched off. If it is 'on' then the device knows that another one is transmitting. If 'off' then it first switches it on and then transmits. Collisions can occur as in an ordinary implementation of CSMA/CD, so a listening mechanism is required to detect this.

The transmission rate for Cluster/One is 240 Kbps and the total cable lengths can be around 300m, arranged as a branching bus, without loops. The maximum number of devices permitted is 64, but two networks can be interlinked by a gateway, again an Apple microcomputer.

The network is marketed as an integrated office system, combining the network, the workstations and a range of user-oriented software packages (electronic mail, word processing, electronic filing and information handling).

6.5.2 Econet (Acorn Computers)

The Econet system, made and marketed by the UK company Acorn Computers, is similar in approach to Cluster/One. Econet is designed

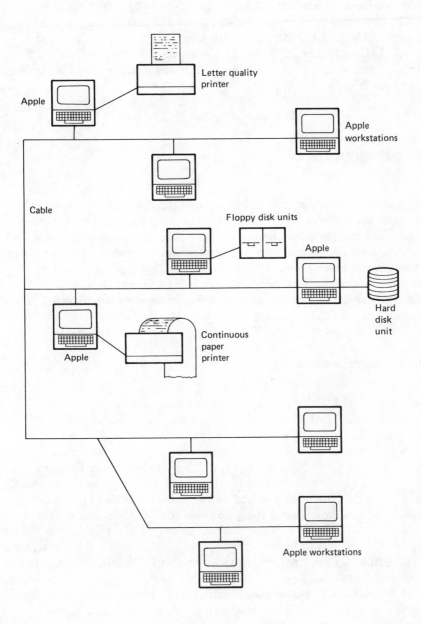

Figure 6.6 Typical NESTAR Cluster/One network

explicitly to link Acorn Atom microcomputers together. It was envisaged as a system for use in the educational environment, but it is adequate for many office applications as well.

The cable is 4-wire twisted pair and up to 255 devices can share the same network. The data transfer rate is 210 Kbps and the maximum length is 1 km. Again a form of CSMA/CD is used, adapted specifically for the limited environment of Acorn Atoms. A shared disk file device is provided, based again on an Acorn Atom.

6.6 OTHER OPTIONS

All the access methods, physical media and topologies described in earlier chapters lend themselves to use for local area networks. Apart from the contention-bus, broadband bus and Cambridge ring systems described so far, the most important commercial techniques are those based on register insertion and token access. Obviously optical fibre is going to be very important as the physical medium when it is freely and cheaply available, or when its use can be justified to meet some very special requirement (light weight, long distance, freedom from electrical interference, etc.).

6.6.1 Register Insertion

The Swiss-based telecommunications equipment company Hasler has designed and is marketing a register insertion ring called SILK (System for Integrated Local Communications). The technique of register insertion has been fully explained in chapter 5. Hasler's current SILK implementation of it uses the third technique described, that is, with the sender putting a packet of data on to the ring and with the receiver removing it. To ensure that the packets are acknowledged properly, higher levels of protocol have been used, based on normal standards used for public data networks.

Hasler's SILK holds a unique position among local area networks since it was one of the first to be operational in an experimental system. It was also developed by a company more closely associated with telecommunications than with computing.

In the early 1970s Hasler started serious experiments on digital telephones for use on a single site. They developed a simple ring-shaped network which was suitable for carrying both digitised voice traffic and computer-generated data. The laboratory version transported data at 10 Mbps. Uppermost in the minds of the designers was the belief that a single communications network should be incorporated into office buildings, rather than having a separate network for each different application: one for telephones, one for each computer, one for process control, one for alarm systems, etc. By using digital techniques, they reasoned, it should be possible to use a single system to convey all this type of information much more cheaply.

The development of their system was strongly influenced by a number of other developments in computing and electronics. These were

- users of computing and process control equipment were demanding a much more flexible switching system than they had been accustomed to, so that they could interconnect their devices more freely;
- there was a big price drop in LSI circuits, especially microprocessors, memories and digital codec chips (used to digitise analogue voice signals) —this resulted in better software in the devices using and incorporated into the network, since the use of available hardware no longer needed to be minimised;
- it became cost effective to manufacture customised integrated circuits suitable for use at high frequencies—these were essential for transmitting digital data at high speeds.

Much emphasis has been placed on SILK's 'integrated' aspects. It has, therefore, been designed to provide uniform facilities for data, telegraphy, telephone, etc.

On the technical side, SILK is a ring network in which data can travel in one direction only. The current system operates at 16 Mbps and uses standard 75 ohm coaxial cable with baseband signalling. One of its most important features from the point of view of the prospective customer is its use of standard telecommunications protocols for attaching devices. Thus, a customer uses the same protocols for connecting to SILK as he would for a public data network.

A typical SILK ring is shown in figure 6.7. Devices are normally attached to the network through their nearest local block (LBL in the figure). Up to 150 local blocks are allowed on the network, each of which can support several individual devices. The end devices themselves are connected through the same interface devices as would be used for connection to a public digital network.

One main block (MBL) is needed for each network; this performs the usual ring network monitoring and housekeeping functions. The presence and operation of a main block is essential, so it may be duplicated in practice. The main block can also perform as a local block by allowing end devices to attach to the network.

Local blocks (and the main blocks) are interconnected by coaxial or optical fibre cables using a duplicated 'braided' system. In this each local

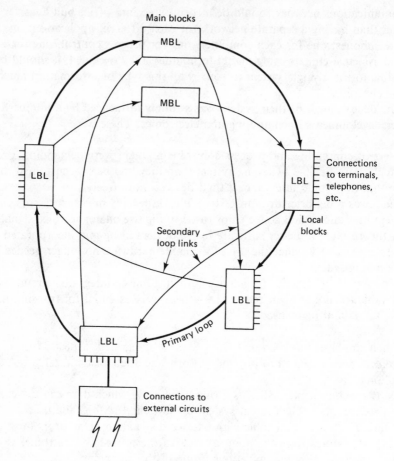

Figure 6.7 SILK ring structure

block is attached directly to its immediate neighbours by one cable (the primary loop) and to the next ones directly by the other cable (the secondary loop) as shown in figure 6.7. Thus, if a link or a local block fails, the alternative link can be used to bypass the failed section. A tertiary loop is also possible.

SILK is designed to handle voice traffic as well as data. The telephones used are special Hasler devices with a built-in digitiser and many other features. A caller on one of these telephones can dial another telephone on the network, and the conversation is handled by means of packets of digitised speech being transmitted from one to the other. The call set-up does not require a central telephone exchange since the telephones themselves, together with their associated local blocks and the SILK addressing scheme, are capable of handling all the necessary functions. A normal exchange is required to handle calls to and from the external public telephone network. The ring uses small packets with up to 16 bytes of data to transmit information.

6.6.2 Token Access

Token-access techniques can be used on rings or buses. PRIME Computers implemented, as part of their PRIMENET networking system, a token-passing loop for interconnecting their computers within a limited geographical area. Other portions of PRIMENET handled communications between the computers and terminals over longer distances.

Apollo Computers also market a token-passing ring for their DOMAIN (Distributed Operating MultiAccess Interactive Network) system. This is an integrated set of hardware and software products intended for the engineering and design environment. Each user has a personal computer system which is linked to others in order to share resources. The ring uses conventional coaxial cable to link the systems and operates at a transmission speed of 12 Mbps. The operation of the token-passing mechanism and the method of access are quite conventional and have been explained in detail in Chapter 5.

Token-passing buses are much more complex to implement successfully, although the technique does exhibit several advantages over other systems. The problems of implementation are concerned mainly with the techniques used for devices to enter and to leave a logical sequence and also with ensuring that only one token is in use at any given time.

REFERENCE

1 Digital Equipment Corporation, Intel Corporation and Xerox Corporation, *The Ethernet: A Local Area Network Data Link Layer and Physical Layer Specification*, DEC, Intel and Xerox, September 1980 (obtainable from Xerox Corporation, OPD Systems Development, 3450 Hillview Avenue, Palo Alto, CA 94304, USA).

7 Performance Characteristics

The average purchaser of a local area network is generally looking for a value-for-money solution to his immediate problems. If the network can also increase the quality of the work done and make it easier for the user to do his job better then this is a welcome bonus. Not all the experimental local area networks were designed with performance as a prime consideration. The Cambridge ring, for example, had so much more communication bandwidth available than traditional computer networks that during its initial design phase no attempt was made to optimise its use [1].

The Cambridge ring can be said to perform well in that, under normal circumstances, data can be moved from one device attached to the network to another in a very short time with a high end-to-end transfer rate over extended periods of time and with few errors. However, the amount of information moved in each ring slot is only 16 bits out of a total of 38 bits or more. The remainder of the slot is used for ring control purposes. This is hardly an efficient mode of transport when considered at this level, but it obviously performs adequately for most purposes.

The Cambridge ring is being used here as an example of the factors involved in considering the performance of a local area network. Other networking techniques show similar features, with a trade-off having been made at some stage in their development between cost, ease of implementation, data-transmission rate, error rate and intended method of use.

When it comes to actually marketing a system the criteria used to evaluate performance could well be different. For example, the network may be needed to serve a very large population of terminals and personal workstations where raw data-transfer speed is unimportant but where a low network delay and the ability to support a large number of users simultaneously are paramount.

In this chapter the main factors affecting performance are discussed. Local area networks pose special problems for monitoring and measuring performance. These are also discussed in some detail. Finally, one of the appealing features of local area networks has been the apparent freedom that they give to the user in respect of adding new devices from a number of sources. This, together with other forms of upgrading, are examined to see just how the local area networks in existence match up to expectations.

7.1 FACTORS DETERMINING PERFORMANCE

Performance of any system, whether it is a mainframe computer, a microcomputer or a network, is very subjective. What suits one class of user may be thought inefficient by another class. What suits the end-user of a network may be uneconomic or difficult to implement by its designers.

Performance will be treated in this section under the following headings:

Throughput
The attached device
The end-user
Error types and error rates
Ability to obtain access to the network
Techniques for achieving reliability

7.1.1 Throughput

Throughput is one of the most important factors in network performance as seen by the user. It is the amount of data that the network can transport between the attached devices. Figure 7.1 shows throughput plotted against the load presented to the network for various possibilities.

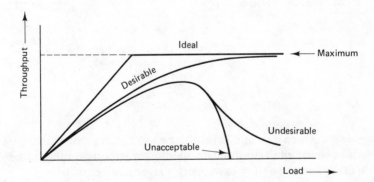

Figure 7.1 Possible network throughput characteristics

Ideal This is what every designer should aim to provide. The throughput increases steadily with the load presented until it reaches its maximum possible value, where it remains however much more the load increases.
Desirable This is a practical alternative to the ideal situation. The network

throughput increases with the applied load and gradually approaches the maximum value.

Undesirable This is also a practical possibility but not one which users would like to encounter. The throughput increases with load to peak at some value less than the maximum possible, and then falls as the load is increased further.

Unacceptable No practical implementation should be made with these characteristics. The throughput rises to a peak below the theoretical maximum and then falls to zero when the load reaches a certain critical point. At this point the network becomes deadlocked and no further increase in load will result in any data passing through it.

Most local area networks tend towards the 'desirable' situation although some early implementations before the techniques were developed exhibited the 'undesirable' and 'unacceptable' characteristics.

Figure 7.2 shows the major elements that affect the throughput of a network, assuming that the attached devices have already prepared the information for transmission by putting it in packets.

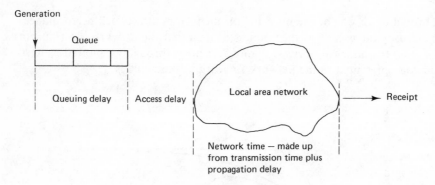

Figure 7.2 Delays in transmission

Queuing delay Once a packet is ready to be sent it must be placed in a queue in a network interface device behind other packets waiting to be transmitted.

Access delay A packet at the head of the queue will usually have to wait for a convenient opportunity in the existing network traffic before it can be transmitted. This can either be a gap between packets in transit, a quiet interval on the network, after a time-out period if the previous transmission was lost or corrupted, or when that access point is given permission to transmit.

Transmission time A certain finite time is required to transmit all the contents of the packet on to the network. This is a function of the modulation rate or signalling speed of the network, and the operating speed of the interface unit. Typical networks operate in the region of 1–10 Mbps.

Propagation delay Every signal on the network travels through it at a high, but finite, speed. A radio transmission in a vacuum travels at the speed of light. Electrical signals through copper wire are slower. Thus, the packet takes a finite time to reach its destination.

Once the information reaches its destination it is checked and analysed by the receiving network interface device and then passed on to the attached end-user device or application software.

The queuing delay can be an important restriction on the perceived network speed, especially when the device being used is capable of generating long streams of data over a short period, or when the network is congested. If the packet is unable to be transmitted quickly once it reaches the head of the queue, it is possible that the queue could overfill. Some procedure is necessary to prevent the source of the data from attempting to put more packets in a queue that is already full.

In general, ring access schemes are predictable and are very unlikely to cause the whole network to become deadlocked. The reason is obvious: permission to transmit is normally required on a ring (either explicitly with tokens, or implicitly with other techniques). This is relatively easy to control and generally permission passes sequentially round the ring. Bus networks that operate by giving each device permission in some manner are equally easy to predict.

Predicting performance on bus networks that employ contention-access techniques is a major problem for the user and designer. These techniques rely on the average conditions over a period giving devices equal opportunities to use the network.

Consider first the contention-bus networks. On a bus the signal is transmitted by one device and it is propagated to all points in the network, after which it dies away naturally. The time that it takes the signal to reach all parts of the network is critical, since it is during this period that other users may not be aware that the network is already in use, and hence they may themselves transmit. The traffic-carrying capacity of the network is a function of the network propagation time for contention systems. Figure 7.3 shows the general trends for a hypothetical contention-access method, but one that is typical of those in common use. Pure and slotted ALOHA systems are also shown for comparison, but these are constant. Concise discussions of the problems of network delay and its effect on broadcast systems, with particular reference to ALOHA and CSMA techniques, are contained in references [2] and [3].

As the network delay increases, so does the time taken for a signal to reach all extremities of the network. A CSMA/CD system must be able to detect the presence of another signal while actually transmitting, so the

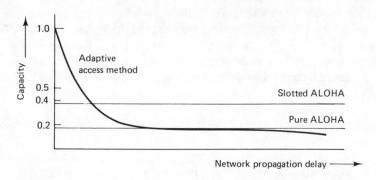

Figure 7.3 Network capacity plotted against propagation delay

packets should be long enough to be still in transmission after the signal has reached the whole of the network. Figure 7.4a shows a network with a particular minimum packet size and network delay. Stations A and B are at the maximum separation and a packet from B arrives at A before A has finished transmitting. Similarly for B. Thus both A and B know that their packets are being corrupted, so they abandon transmission and try again later. Figure 7.4b shows the same two stations but with the network delay increased. A finishes transmission before B's packet arrives. Thus it does not realise that it is likely to be corrupted before it reaches its destination. Figure 7.4c shows the possible result at another station on the network that hears both the packets from A and B overlapping. In a practical implementation a higher-level protocol than that used in the access method would be needed to detect a lost packet and request retransmission.

In order to avoid the possibility described above, on a contention-bus system a minimum packet size is required which is a function of the maximum network delay. As the delay increases, possibly because the network length increases, so the minimum packet size must be increased. For small fixed-size messages this generally involves the packet overheads being increased, which in turn use up more network capacity.

If the transmission rate of one of these networks is increased, the time for which a packet is in existence on the network is decreased. This has the same effect as lengthening the network.

The problems of throughput are different for rings and are generally much easier to predict regardless of the method of access. Practically every viable ring access technique for local area networks uses a sequential mode of access. Devices can transmit only at a suitable gap between packets in transit or when specifically given permission.

Ring capacity is normally measured as the raw data-transmission rate, which is the rate at which packets are transferred between points on the ring. The actual end-to-end information transfer rate between terminals,

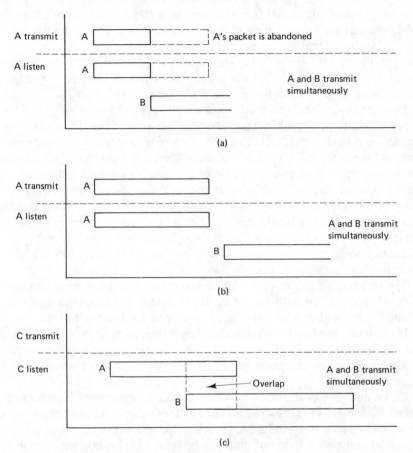

Figure 7.4 Effects of long network transmission delays on detection over packet overlap. (a) Network propagation delay short enough for A to detect packet corruption. (b) Network propagation delay too great for packet from B to reach A before A finishes transmission. (c) Same packets from A and B as in (b), but as heard in station C intermediate between A and B

programs or human users can be much lower. The Cambridge ring, for example, normally runs at 10 Mbps, but this is only the rate at which the slot circulates round the ring. A slot cannot be used continuously by one station for transmission since all the other stations must be given an equal opportunity to transmit. Thus, if the ring has only one slot and a station is transmitting a string of data to another, it will use the slot for a portion of the string, then release the slot for someone else. The station can only use the slot again when the slot is next passed to it flagged as 'empty'. If no other stations are needing the slot it will circulate once round the ring empty (assuming that the monitor station does not use it to test ring integrity) before the transmitting station can use it again. If other stations are also transmitting, the slot will circulate several times before it will again be available to the station being considered here.

Even if the slot could be used continuously, only a portion of the capacity would be available, since about 60 per cent of the slot is used for address and control fields, leaving around 40 per cent for user information. Some of the slot is used by the destination device to acknowledge in various ways the correct receipt or otherwise of the slot. This acknowledgement field has to be checked by the sender for each slot before it can decide whether to send the next part of the message or resend the previous slot. It cannot, therefore, always fill the next empty slot that is passed to it. In practice, if n slots are in transit on the ring, a single station can only transmit once every $(n + 2)$ slots (assuming that no other station has already used that slot).

The maximum point-to-point data transfer rate possible is approximately $4/(n + 2)$ Mbps, for a 10 Mbps ring [1, 4]. For $n = 1$ this gives a rate of about 1.3 Mbps. For $n = 2$ the rate is lower, and is around 1 Mbps.

If the total speed of the Cambridge ring is increased, the total capacity of the network increases in proportion because the number of slots in transit increases. However, the point-to-point performance does not improve at the same rate.

Techniques can be devised to take advantage of this extra capacity. For example, if more slots are used it is not as important to release one as soon as it is returned to the sender. A so-called *slot retention* option can be added so that a long string of data can be transmitted using the same slot continuously over a period of time. Extra levels of acknowledgement above the ring protocol are needed to ensure that this works correctly and errors are handled properly. Another option available is to use a mixture of different sizes of slot. Small slots can be used in the normal manner, each one being emptied immediately it returns to the sender, and long ones can be retained for an extended period to transmit large quantities of information. With both of these techniques higher point-to-point transfer rates can be achieved. The monitor needs to perform extra functions to prevent a slot from being 'retained' forever, and more complex higher-level protocols are needed to perform adequate error checking and flow control.

The standard implementation of the empty slot technique, typified by the Cambridge ring, always guarantees that every device will get an equal share of the capacity of the network.

Register insertion and token-passing rings operate slightly differently from empty slot rings. In both the former techniques a shift register equal to the length of the packet being transmitted is inserted in series with the ring by the sender. This increases the total time that a signal takes to traverse the whole ring so, in effect, the ring increases in size as the number and sizes of the packets in transit increase. The result is that, as the load increases on the network, the effective point-to-point transmission rate decreases. As soon as the load is reduced the rate increases. There is no possibility of a deadlock situation occurring. If the ring point-to-point transfer rate increases, then the end-to-end flow control mechanism will make the sender reduce the rate at which it transmits packets, thereby automatically regulating the load on the network. All the devices are still able to gain access at reasonable intervals regardless of the load.

Token systems have been claimed to provide better utilisation of the network capacity than empty slot rings. Because token-passing and register insertion systems are similar in operation, it is reasonable to expect them to have similar performance characteristics. Possibly the register insertion technique could be slightly better because it does not need to carry the extra overhead of the token, but practical implementations of register insertion rings have used smaller packets on the ring with the result that there is a relatively low data-to-overhead ratio.

As well as the point-to-point data-transfer rate possible on the network, other factors have to be taken into account when assessing throughput. The most important of these is the processing time and protocol overheads involved in providing an information transmission service between users, terminals and applications software. A long message exchange usually involves a high-level protocol which first sets up a liaison without actually exchanging any information relevant to the user. Hence, some transmission time is used for data other than that generated by the user.

In any network some capacity is wasted or not available to be used. The instance of the corrupted transmissions on a contention bus is one obvious example, but in a network in which high data-transmission rates are available it is very likely that the destination device will become 'deaf' to incoming transmissions for short periods. Deafness of a device could be caused by a number of factors, for example:

- no buffers are available for incoming data,
- device is not switched from the transmitting state to the receiving state,
- a preceding packet is still being processed,
- system is not listening because an attached device is not available,
- a failure has occurred,
- device is not switched on.

Allowance for deaf devices must be made by the protocols in use on the network. The Cambridge ring allows for them in the ring-transmission technique by the provision of the acknowledgement (response) field in the slot. A deaf device can either ignore the slot completely or set the field to indicate that it has been rejected. Other local area network techniques usually require an extra level of protocol to acknowledge the receipt of whole packets or messages. The design of the high-level protocols can certainly be simplified if an acknowledgement procedure is built in to the lower levels of the access method. Simple high-level protocols generally improve the overall throughput possible with the network by reducing the processing required in the interface or attached devices.

7.1.2 The Attached Device

The attached device referred to here is the equipment associated with the end-user. It could be a terminal, workstation, computer system or any other piece of equipment that provides information to the network rather than being involved in the mechanism of transporting it.

In general, the attached devices will spend some time processing a packet of information before actually transmitting it, or after having received it from elsewhere. A typical message or piece of information will be too long for the ordinary packet transmitted on the network. This is especially true with empty slot rings, and also to a certain extent with register insertion and token-passing rings because of the electronic circuits and shift registers needed in their operation. Packet sizes for contention-bus systems are less restricted, although a packet that is too long can cause unnecessary delays for the other users. Thus a message for transmission must usually be split up into portions that can fit inside the packets used. Each packet must have the appropriate header information filled in, together with the address of the destination device, and possibly the destination program or terminal attached to that device in situations where more than one is possible (for example, multiprogramming computers and device multiplexers).

Once a packet has been prepared for transmission it must be placed in a buffer queue along with other packets awaiting transmission. The network interface device then sends the packets one by one, when it gets the opportunity.

On receipt of a packet from another device the contents generally need to be checked against the check fields in the trailer; if any errors are detected a message has to be sent to the sender of the erroneous packet requesting retransmission. It is more usual to ignore erroneous packets and only acknowledge those correctly received. The lack of an acknowledgement can then be taken as an implicit request for retransmission. If the packet has no detectable errors, its sequence number has to be checked so that missing packets can be detected. Eventually the whole message can be reassembled from the individual portions. If more than one end device or program are attached to the interface unit the packets or messages have to be sent to the appropriate destination.

Further levels of protocol may be required to provide other functions. For example, an exchange of information is needed between a terminal and a host computer system in order that the host may determine the characteristics of the terminal. Then the terminal user has to establish what service is required and the service has to verify that this user is known to it and is allowed to access the system. The number of tasks to be performed will vary with the system and with the application being used. All of these functions involve the exchange of data, which is subsequently processed, before the information transfer can begin.

7.1.3 The End-user

To a terminal user, the response that the network gives is the most important factor in determining its performance. As has been seen, this response is the sum of the response provided by the application or service being accessed, the network response itself and the protocol processing necessary to ensure that the right user accesses the right information and gets the message required in the right order, etc. The network view of this exchange is totally different. All the network sees is one string of bits followed by another, each string having no meaning to it.

Certain classes of end-user demand different qualities of service. The terminal user referred to above usually demands a quick response to requests made from the terminal. Since a typical terminal can respond only at a low speed (up to a few hundred bits per second), the fact that the network is capable of handling several millions bits per second may seem unimportant. What is more important to the user is the ability to send a message more or less immediately, and for the destination system to respond quickly. A high data-transmission rate on the network is needed to provide this level of response if several hundred terminals are using it. If a network, or a channel on that network, has to support fewer devices, then a slower data-transmission speed will provide the same level of response. This is one reason why a single cable baseband network needs to operate at high speed. A single cable using a frequency-division multiplexed broadband system can allocate a number of relatively low-speed channels each to a few devices, although the whole network can still support as many or more than a baseband system.

On the other hand a computer system accessing a file on a remote device or other computer system requires a different type of service from the network. The file may be very long, so the quicker it is transferred the better, in order that resources in the sender and destination systems can be released. Obviously a high point-to-point transfer rate is important for this type of application, although the speed of response will be less critical.

Some industrial process-control systems demand a quick response combined with a high data-transmission rate, particularly in situations with interlinked monitoring and processing devices. A particular condition detected in one process may need to be reported to another device so that appropriate action can be taken elsewhere.

All end-users, or items of applications software, have their own particular set of requirements in terms of network performance.

7.1.4 Error Types and Error Rates

Errors introduced by networks in which packets are being transmitted fall into the following categories

Damaged   Information is actually corrupted by the network during transmission owing to noise or collisions with other packets. Noise is a problem common to all networks, although local area networks exhibit considerably less than most wide area networks. Packets that are corrupted by colliding with others are a problem found only with packet broadcast systems, and these are common for local area networks, mainly CSMA systems. Special techniques are not needed to detect collisions since the error checking used for protocols like high-level data link control (HDLC) is generally perfectly adequate.

Lost   Packets can be 'lost' in any packet-switched network if the address field is altered by noise. It is then delivered to the wrong destination or discarded. On a local area network, if the device whose address appears in the packet header is not listening then that packet is ignored by everybody. Generally an acknowledgement procedure is built into high-level protocols which either demands that each packet be acknowledged individually, or ensures that those missing from a sequence can be detected.

Duplicated   If an acknowledgement gets lost, the sender of the packet must assume that it was not delivered or was in error. Hence, it might transmit the same packet twice. Most protocols have procedures built in to detect and discard duplicate packets.

Out of sequence   When a message is made up from several packets, and one or more are lost or damaged in transmit, then the packets received may be in a different order from those originally set up for transmission. Before passing on the complete message it is usual for the software to put the packets back in sequence.

Most of these errors are handled by protocols at a higher level than the actual local area network access method. Since local area networks generally introduce few errors in the actual transmission, the techniques can be quite crude but still effective.

The technique used on the Cambridge ring illustrates a simple, but effective method. Each slot used on the ring is very small and the repeaters, used to provide access points and regenerate the signal, are close together. Thus it is unlikely that more than one bit in each slot will be changed between one repeater and the next. At the end of the slot a single parity bit is employed which is checked by every repeater. In fact the repeater does not transmit the parity bit it receives, but always transmits the one that it calculates as the slot is read in and transmitted to the next repeater. If the calculated parity bit does not correspond to the parity bit received, the slot must have been in error. The next empty slot that repeater receives is used to transmit an error-reporting message to the monitor station. In this way the monitor can build up a picture of the parts of the ring in which errors are being introduced. Of course, the slot that arrives at the destination (unless the address field is damaged) will be in error. The higher-level protocols used in the Cambridge ring detect the errors in the HDLC type of packet that is used — the basic block protocol. Most other local area networks use this technique as standard.

7.1.5 Ability to Obtain Access to the Network

A network may be able to transport information very quickly from one location to another without introducing many errors, but this is of only limited value to the end-user if he cannot get access to the network when he wants to. Networks that are constructed from point-to-point links between systems generally experience few problems of this kind. The software inside the linked systems could be overloaded at certain times making it difficult for them to handle the volume of information being offered. Network congestion, or apparent congestion, is more a feature of networks in which circuits and network-switching devices are shared by all the users. Generally, the network capacity is determined by the typical maximum amount of traffic carried rather than by the absolute maximum that the users could present.

Local area networks provide transmission facilities for a large number of potential users, so occasional problems with capacity can be expected, although by no means all are caused by the network itself being overloaded.

An attached device may not be able to transmit immediately the information that it has ready to send for a number of reasons. Some of the most significant are as follows

Network interface   The device or portion of the equipment responsible for accessing the network may be able to handle only a limited number of attached devices at any one time, even though a greater number of user devices or items of software may be attached. Also buffer space in the interface may be limited and, with some techniques, the return of the original packet, or an acknowledgement, may be required before the buffer can be freed.

Access method   The technique used to gain access to the network may be slow or unfair. A slow technique is most likely to result from a heavily loaded transmission system and may be the way in which the load on it is regulated to prevent a more serious overload. Some access methods can be unfair under certain circumstances, although with the techniques in common use this is unlikely to be noticeable to the end-user except in circumstances where the network as a whole is seriously overloaded. Then, as the amount of information presented is reduced to match the available capacity, the situation generally eases. Other local area networking techniques, particularly those used for ring-shaped networks, are inherently fair. A high load will result in a slower end-to-end transport of information, with each user getting an equal share. Even then, the data-transfer rate will be more than most attached devices can handle. In general, the access method itself does not cause significant hold-ups to the end-user trying to obtain access to the network.

Protocols   Between the two end-users or applications involved in an exchange of information a protocol is needed to ensure an orderly and correct flow of data. Naturally, the more sophisticated the end-to-end protocol, the more time it takes to perform its functions. Error checking, sequence checking and flow control can take up a significant amount of time if they are performed thoroughly.

7.2 TECHNIQUES FOR ACHIEVING RELIABILITY

Reliability is a measure of the extent to which the network or system performs in the expected manner. A local area network may involve a large number of users all of whom depend to some extent on the network performing properly. Because of this, special techniques are usually employed to ensure a high degree of reliability.

Reliability affects the availability of the network, that is, the ratio of the time during which the network is working to the time when it is not. The network may not fail completely when it develops a fault but may give a slower throughput, may introduce errors or may give a degraded service. The extent to which the network service can be degraded before it becomes unacceptable varies with the different users' perceptions of the system. If a network degrades by reducing its normal end-to-end information transfer speed, this may not be very noticeable to the ordinary user, although the proportion of the usable capacity of the network may be reduced significantly. This may become apparent only when the load is high.

With most local area networking techniques, each transceiver, repeater or other form of network interface usually performs the network-access and time-division multiplexing (if this is used) independently of the others on the network. So one device accessing the network more slowly than normal will not usually affect the running of the other devices. A device that actually degrades in such a way that it transmits at a different rate from all the other devices will upset the whole network since its data will not be readable by the others. Some systems, in particular rings, will then cease operation altogether. With other networks the offending device will not be able to converse with others, although the rest of the system will continue to operate in the normal manner; this latter situation is more typical of shared-baseband bus systems using a CSMA or similar access method.

Various faults in individual devices can develop which can affect the whole of a local area network. Those most commonly encountered are in the ring-shaped networks in which the repeaters or other devices play an active part in transmitting the information between locations. If one of these devices fails then it is going to prevent information from flowing through it properly. Since this is a critical component in a ring, and since it is so important that a local area network must continue to operate, at least in a degraded form, even though parts of it may be performing incorrectly or not at all, various techniques have been developed to avoid the problems. Typically, these are

Independent power supplies for the repeater The repeater itself is really part of the network rather than part of the attached device, so it should be as independent of the end-user devices as possible. One way of achieving this is to power it separately from the attached device so that the latter can be switched off, unplugged, etc. without affecting the operation of the network. One way is for the repeater to obtain its power directly from the cables that are used for transferring the information; then one or more power supplies can be provided for the whole network, and these are always switched on while the network is running.

Repeater can be bypassed when it has no power Alternatively the repeaters may incorporate a switching relay. When its power is removed this relay switches the ring transmission circuit to bypass the repeater rather than passing through it. The repeater can obviously share the power supply of the attached device.

This may seem an ideal solution to the problem of ensuring continued operation of the ring regardless of the state of the attached devices. If a repeater fails it can just be switched off and the ring can then resume operation, although the devices attached to the ring through the failed repeater would not be able to participate. There are some problems, however. Most ring systems rely on the repeaters being reasonably close together so that the signal can be regenerated before it becomes too weak or distorted by the transmission medium. Thus, when a repeater is bypassed the distance between adjacent *operating* repeaters will be increased in this section. If two adjacent repeaters are bypassed the distance is increased still further. Thus the technique is not very suitable for systems in which the repeaters must be close together, or where devices are liable to be switched off.

Contention-baseband bus networks, in which all the devices share the same channel, do not require repeaters to the same extent, except to link two separate bus segments. The attached devices are connected to the bus through interface devices and transceivers. If one of these fails then only the devices attached to it directly are affected. The only way in which a bus interface or transceiver could fail and affect the whole network would be if one transmitted a continuous signal or incorrect packets. The solution is simple: just switch it off.

Broadband networks use the same sort of access techniques and modems as normal data-transmission systems, so the reliability is similar. Remote diagnostic devices can easily be incorporated so that a supervisor can check the state of all the interfaces to the network from one location. The transmission repeaters, amplifiers, splitters, taps and cables used for broadband networks are, in general, standard off-the-shelf cable television products which are built for very long life in arduous conditions.

7.3 MONITORING PERFORMANCE

Traditional types of data-transmission networks have generally incorporated a monitoring device of some description in order to understand how the network is performing under normal operating conditions. Sometimes the monitoring function can be carried out quite successfully by an existing processor in the network.

Monitoring operating conditions is often thought of only after the network has been installed and has been running for some time. Then, possibly the organisation decides that the network is to be extended or to have more traffic put on it, but before that can be done it is necessary to know typical traffic flows and loads. Sometimes the network does not perform in practice as its designers expected, so the traffic must be monitored to discover the reason.

The need for monitoring, and the parameters to be measured, should be recognised *before* the network is installed. Local area networks are little different in this respect, although the way that traffic is monitored may not be the same owing to the transmission speed of the network and because it covers a limited geographical area. Experience has shown that local area networks generally have a very low error rate when compared with some other data-transmission networks. Also, link failures are rare and the bandwidth available is more than adequate to meet the requirements of the users. In a local area network the cost of using the network is not often charged directly to the users, although the external circuits that are employed to access other sites may be.

Thus, a monitor of a local area network will need to measure parameters associated with ensuring that the network performs properly rather than with obtaining traffic statistics for charging purposes. The following items are typical

Load   Although the capacity of most local area networks appears to be considerably in excess of the current requirements of the users, it is valuable to measure the load on the system, especially when it is planned to add new devices and applications. Some systems can degrade quite noticeably at loads well below the quoted maximum, so it is advisable to realise when these loads are being approached in order that measures can be taken to meet them.

Traffic information   It is useful to know how much traffic is passing between various devices on the network, how much is destined for devices on external networks and how many packets have to be retransmitted owing to errors or the destination devices not listening. If external networks are accessed via the local area network then the devices using the external circuits, and the quantity of information transmitted, will normally have to be measured so that the appropriate users are charged.

Failures   Failures in a local area network can involve the network access devices, repeaters, transceivers, modems and, less often, the interconnecting medium itself (including the cables and connectors). Broadband networks also use a headend device to receive and retransmit all the signals, either on a different cable or on a different frequency. The network monitoring device should be able to detect components of the network that have failed or that are degrading the service. The technique used in implementations of the Cambridge ring is one example of the way that the monitor can be used to detect errors in the repeaters. Its operation has already been described. Bus networks do not require repeaters or transceivers to report errors explicitly as the monitor itself is able to hear every transmission that is made.

Bottlenecks   On early computer networks in which single circuits linked individual processors, some links were subjected to higher loads than others. This could be important especially where one link was used by several computer systems. In such cases overloading on that link would hold up all processors using the link. Most local area networks use a shared circuit so there is only one circuit in which a bottleneck can occur. However, in broadband networks using several separate channels a bottleneck may occur in one channel while the others remain relatively free. If this situation persists then it may make sense to transfer some traffic from this channel to another. Bottlenecks on local area networks are more likely to occur in the interface devices used to link the computers, terminals and workstations to the network. Very often a single interface device performs as a terminal concentrator, and if too many terminals are trying to send at the same time the device could be overloaded. It is difficult to monitor this directly from a remote location, although the interface could measure it itself and report to the monitor every so often.

Because of the high data-transmission rates normally employed on local area networks, it is difficult for any single device to monitor, analyse and store all the traffic on the network when it is fully loaded. A filtering technique is essential to extract a representative selection of the traffic or to monitor only specific types of information or conditions. The monitor, in common with monitoring devices on other types of network, must also be able to exist and do its work without affecting the normal traffic flows. Some monitors can also be configured to provide error-correction facilities — the Cambridge ring being a well-known example. Monitors can use quiet periods on any type of local area network to send out diagnostic messages to determine the state of the network or any component of it.

In addition to the normal monitoring functions, the device employed can act as a traffic simulator for making tests of capacity, error frequency and throughput. A traffic simulator cannot possibly simulate every possible condition on the network, but it is a useful tool to have when testing, designing or tuning the network. In particular a certain condition can be simulated and if this requires further investigation it can easily be repeated or slightly altered using a simulator. This would be impossible to control under normal operating conditions.

The use of monitors and traffic simulations allows the designer and owner of a network to predict performance and validate certain design features. On networks with optional facilities these can be tested and their effects measured before actually deciding to implement them on the final version.

7.4 UPGRADING AND MODIFYING THE NETWORK

Seldom, if ever, are computer systems installed that remain exactly in that form for a significant period of time. Users find either that the system does not perform as well as expected and so they find other ways of doing things, or that the system can assist them in other tasks that were not planned for. Networks are prime examples of the way requirements change. Typically, users require more speed, because they are moving more data than they thought they would or they are not satisfied with the transmission speed they get. Users often find the network so useful that they add more devices and use it for other purposes with the result that the capacity available becomes insufficient. New devices may be introduced that require different interfaces to the network.

One of the original ideas behind local area networks was that there would be more than enough capacity available to handle the communication needs within a site. Implicit in this was the concept that only communications between normal digital devices would be involved. However, this is only one of the forms of information that is communicated. In addition to digital data there is voice traffic in analogue or digital form, facsimile information and possibly visual information. Many of the local area networks that have been developed are unsuitable for analogue signals in any form, nor do they have the capacity to handle more than a few digitised telephone conversations simultaneously. Other systems can easily do so, and consequently they are far easier to upgrade in terms of capacity.

Local area networks generally have a very simple topology with the minimum of cable. The cable can often be installed throughout the building or site close to most areas in which devices that will use the network will be placed. Thus, the need to put an extra length of cable in, or to divert an existing one, is minimised. In cases where the topology has to be altered for some reason the usual problems of rerouteing data communications cables are experienced: new ducts, preferred routes already occupied, need to cut cable and join new sections, etc. The cost of installation of any cable run is likely to exceed the cost of the cable itself.

Some local area networking techniques are particularly sensitive to excessive cable lengths. A Cambridge ring using twisted-pair cable, for example, performs best if the distance between repeaters is quite short. Most other ring systems have similar requirements. Ethernet and other baseband bus systems impose a maximum cable length for the whole network which depends on the packet size, transmission speed and signalling technique used. Broadband networks have very few restrictions on capacity, cable length or topology, provided that there are no closed loops in the system.

Generally, local area networks are not easy to upgrade in terms of speed or capacity once they have been installed. For example, if a 10 Mbps network is insufficient for the needs of the user it would necessitate changing every transceiver, controller and repeater in the network to increase its speed.

Increasing the speed of a baseband contention-bus network also has important implications on the minimum packet size that can be transmitted and on the total length of the bus. As explained in an earlier section, the higher the transmission speed used, the longer must be the minimum packet size allowed and the shorter the total bus length, in order that all the devices on the network can hear the transmission before the sender has finished, so that packet collisions can be reliably detected.

Most ring networks operate in baseband mode and increasing the speed requires all the ring repeaters to be changed. A higher speed will allow more or larger packets to circulate. Some ring networks use fixed-length packets for transport; others use packets of variable length. Changing the length of the packets in a fixed-length system can have serious repercussions on the electronic hardware in the repeaters. However, the length of the network using the ring technique is easy to alter without having any serious impact on the data-transmission characteristics. A longer ring naturally means that the information will take longer to travel completely round the network, but advantage can be taken of this by using more or longer packets. Altering the technique employed in a ring, from empty slot to register insertion or token passing for example, can be relatively simple, but it depends largely on the internal design of the repeaters themselves. The access logic employed also needs modification. As an example, the University of Cambridge Computer Laboratory changed from using a register insertion system to the present empty slot technique. The repeaters at that time were all hand-built from discrete components and the change from one technique to the other was relatively easy.

Broadband networks have such a wide bandwidth available that it is most unlikely that normal on-site data communications traffic will use all of it. If the network is also used for some application requiring high bandwidth then the space available for other purposes will be reduced. For example, a real-time colour television channel generally requires 6–8 MHz of bandwidth. This is for a single direction of flow: from transmitter to receivers. A two-way channel would require double this. Although the need for many colour television channels on a local area network is likely to be small, new developments in technology and office techniques could change this situation very quickly.

Considering data transmission only, the design and speed of the modem used on broadband networks is the most important factor. Modems capable of operating on a local area network at 2 Mbps are available, although the current demand for them is low and their cost is relatively high. Most users are content with the throughput that they can get from lower-speed devices using contention (CSMA/CD) channels with a restricted number of users. If more users are needed on a broadband network, more channels can be allocated with little difficulty. Each channel operates on different frequencies from all the others and consequently they are essentially independent in all respects. Increasing the load on one channel does not affect the throughput on another. Each of the channels can operate at different speeds using different access and sharing techniques.

Extending the length of a broadband network is also easy. Since the signals being transmitted on it are modulated, once the signal strength falls below an acceptable level it can be amplified using normal cable television line amplifiers. Thus the overall length of a broadband network can be very great. However, if some of the channels are operated in a contention mode, using CSMA/CD for example, restrictions on the cable length are imposed by the transmission speed and packet length in the same way as for baseband contention-bus networks.

Broadband networks are less sensitive to electrical interference and line characteristics than high-speed baseband systems. Thus broadband systems are ideal for use near electrical machinery, where many other techniques would be unusable. The cable can also be tapped and divided into two or more paths with relative ease making it a straightforward task to add new devices or branches in the cable run.

In conclusion, if the network is likely to be modified in shape and length considerably after it is installed, and if it is going to be used for a variety of tasks in addition to the straightforward one of transmitting data, then a broadband system is the best choice. The initial cost will almost certainly be higher than for baseband bus networks or rings, but the user will be getting flexibility, high capacity and the ability to expand its range of uses. Against these advantages must be weighed the fact that more complex interfaces are needed and that the whole network depends on the headend device which receives all the transmissions made by the other devices and retransmits them on another cable or at another frequency. It must be recognised that baseband bus and ring networks are more than adequate for most local data-transmission purposes and can handle very large numbers of devices with no degradation of service.

REFERENCES

1 Wilkes, M. V. and Wheeler, D. J., *The Cambridge Digital Communications Ring*, paper presented at the Local Area Communications Network Symposium, Boston, May 1979.
2 Davies, D. W., Barber, D. L. A., Price, W. L. and Solomonides, C. M., *Computer Networks and their Protocols*, John Wiley, Chichester, 1979.
3 Hayes, J. F., 'Local Distribution in Computer Communications', *IEEE Communications Magazine*, Volume 19 No. 2 (March 1981) 6–14.
4 Hopper, A., 'The Cambridge Ring — A Local Network', in F. K. Hanna (Editor), *Advanced Techniques for Microprocessor Systems*, Peter Peregrinus, Hitchin, Herts., 1980.

8 *Applications for Local Area Networks*

Local area networks are an essential stage in the development of local systems for distributed computing and in the use of electronic devices in the office environment. They offer the customer very significant cost and performance advantages when compared with more traditional data-communication networks. In addition, a local area network can provide a means of interconnecting a large number of devices using a highly reliable network which would be difficult or impossible to achieve any other way at a reasonable cost. Most local networks are easier to extend than other types of network provided, of course, that their extent is confined to the local site and that the overall length does not exceed the maximum allowed for that particular network.

In their most basic form local area networks are only systems for moving information streams from one location to another, but generally users of a network require extra services to be provided to make the network more 'friendly'. It is likely that information generated by the devices on a local area network will sometimes need to be transmitted to devices elsewhere that are not on the local system. To do this special gateway or bridging devices are required to link the local area network to another network or a public system. These gateway devices may be supplied as part of the network. These and other requirements are discussed in the following sections.

8.1 COMPUTER NETWORKS

In its simplest form a computer network is a system of computers, terminals and peripherals linked together in some manner by a series of telecommunications circuits. Applications related to the end-user, as distinct from network and system support processing, may be performed in several processors located in several different positions. This is the normal distributed processing system which was referred to earlier. Another longer-established form of computer network retains most of the processing power in a central location and uses a telecommunications network to allow remote users with terminals to access the central services.

Most computer networks extend over several geographically separate sites and consequently they use circuits belonging to or leased from the national telecommunications authority. In this way they may be thought to be unsuitable for use with local area networks, but a closer examination shows this not to be the case. Most computer networks are similar to the one shown in figure 8.1. A computer at one site typically serves a local

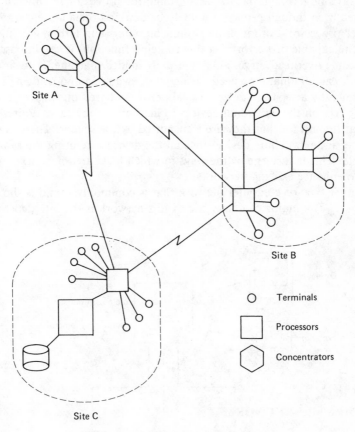

Figure 8.1 Multisite computer network

population of users with terminals. Even where there is no processor on the site (for example, site A), the terminals on that site share one or more public or leased lines to the other sites. A concentrator or multiplexer usually serves the terminals in this situation.

Thus, if we consider one site in isolation a local area network could be used to link the terminals to the concentrator or processor to which the off-site lines are connected. This processor then has to become part of the local area network and the complete computer network. It has to perform a gateway function in converting local protocols and addresses into wide area protocols and addresses for information that has to flow outside the site.

For on-site information flow the network performs as a normal local area network but possibly with some enhancements depending on the application being performed and the type of equipment used. In a normal computer network on a site, say site B in figure 8.1, all of the information flowing from any one terminal has to pass through the processor to which it is attached even though it may ultimately be destined for another terminal, or another processor. Although most minicomputers and terminal controllers are quite capable of performing this routeing function, it can impose an unwelcome overhead on an already heavily loaded machine. A local area network can eliminate the need for network switching and routeing to be performed by a separate device. Local networks based on rings or buses usually rely on the individual devices to hear all the messages addressed to them at the instant that they are transmitted by the sender. There is no need for a separate switching device since all the devices are using the same piece of cable. This is just one of the ways in which local area networks can be used to enhance existing networks.

Another type of computer network that is commonly found is shown in figure 8.2. The major characteristic of this network is the interdependence

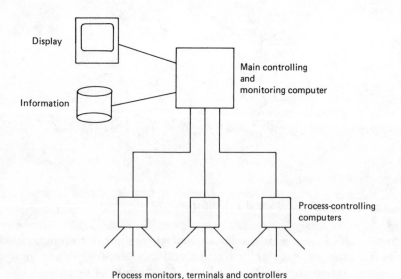

Figure 8.2 Hierarchical process control network

of the computers and other devices.

A typical application is in an industrial manufacturing plant in which various portions of the complete process are controlled by a series of separate computers, monitors, terminals and controllers. A failure in any one of the processes, or in a device controlling the processes, must be notified to a main controlling device which can shut down the plant, inform a supervisor, or automatically shift responsibility for that process on to another device if this is possible. The hierarchical network shown in the figure can easily be transferred to a local area network. The system of hierarchical control can be retained but the wiring can be simplified considerably.

Local area networks can also be used to enhance the service provided by computer networks. Since complete interconnection is the norm for local area networks, and can be achieved in normal computer networks only with difficulty and at a significant cost, the problems of addressing other users on the local network are reduced.

Computer networks are normally built around slow-speed telecommunications circuits which can severely hamper large-scale data transfers between machines. In distributed computing systems there may be several computers in the network equipped with large file-stores. Operating on a file held on a remote computer can involve large numbers of transactions being sent over the network and consequent slow responses on the user's terminal. A common solution to this problem is to copy the file in its entirety to a local processor and then operate on it there, copying it back to the other processor at the end of the update. Local area networks can help alleviate the problem in two ways. Since they operate at a much faster rate than other networks they tend not to be overloaded for most of the time. Hence, it is possible to operate effectively on a remote file provided that the processor on which it is located is connected to the local area network. It is also possible to move files around the network much more rapidly than before.

The interface to a local area network is provided by a single interface device which usually services a single port to the attached device. However, if the attached device is capable of transmitting and receiving data at high speed the interface could service several ports, although 4 or 8 per computer is probably ample.

Computer systems that serve a number of terminals need to provide a port for each terminal, or if multiplexers are used, for each multiplexer. In other words, one port for each incoming line is needed. If the computer system services a large number of lines a large number of ports are needed although most of these will be unused for the majority of the time. A local area network can thus reduce the hardware overhead imposed on a computer system servicing a number of terminals, as well as removing the need for remote multiplexers.

8.2 THE ELECTRONIC OFFICE

Computers, in the form of microprocessors incorporated into otherwise normal equipment, are being increasingly introduced into the office environment. The potential for using computer-based devices in the office is so great that this will become the major market for the next few years and will form the applications for the majority of local area networks installed.

Computerised items of office equipment, in the form of word processors, have been introduced into the office in considerable quantities over the past few years, but this is only one example of the ways that computers and microprocessors can enhance normal office procedures. A few of the more obvious examples will now be discussed briefly, but the reader interested in the details of office technology is referred to the specialised texts listed in references [1] and [2].

The majority of normal office functions can be broken down into four basic activities

Document preparation   This includes the writing and dictation of the original version, typing it, and subsequently modifying, correcting and copying it.

Message distribution   The normal postal service (internal and external), telephoning and travel to and from meetings.

Information management   Handling incoming messages, reports, etc., planning work scheduled, keeping personal diaries, and filing information either temporarily or permanently.

Information access   The use of libraries, standard information services, reference documents, databases and other forms of information.

Electronic equipment is being introduced into the office to serve directly the above tasks. The aim is to help the office worker to perform the routine administrative functions of his job faster and more effectively and so leave more time free for creative thinking. A problem often encountered in the normal office is access to up-to-date information. More time can be spent looking for a report than actually reading it. By using advanced data-handling techniques on a computerised system the task of locating the report and finding if it is relevant could be much easier, to mention just one example.

Another problem commonly encountered in the normal office is contacting another person to obtain information or exchange views, etc. Computer-based mail and telephone-message systems can help considerably here. They cannot, of course guarantee that the person you are trying to contact will be at his desk but various techniques have been devised to ensure that a message can be left for him. Taking the normal telephone call as one example, a sophisticated private telephone exchange can detect that the number dialled has not replied and automatically reroute the call to an alternative number, such as a secretary, who will be able to take the call. This facility has been available for some time from suppliers of private automatic branch telephone exchanges (PABXs). It can be taken one step further in the electronic office. The number called when the original extension does not answer can be a centralised, computer-based service for leaving messages. The caller can leave a short message saying who he is and why he telephoned, and the system will automatically place a message, saying that there are some recorded telephone messages stored away, on the user's electronic messaging system. When the person returns to his office and interrogates the electronic message service, as well as informing him of the electronically stored messages awaiting him, the system will tell him that external telephone calls were made to him and messages were recorded. He can then call a special number to hear them.

Electronic mail is especially useful for messages between individuals in the same organisation. Research has shown that a very large proportion of messages are of this character. By providing each user within the organisation or department with access to a workstation, messages can be written and sent without recourse to a paper copy and the manual postal service.

The above discussion of office-messaging systems, although very brief and incomplete, has indicated that any electronic office scheme requires that the following items be provided

A workstation This is a device similar to a computer visual display unit or terminal but with a limited amount of internal processing capacity. It is linked into a network of other workstations and computerised devices to provide the electronic messaging and information management functions.
Shared facilities To enhance the service provided to individuals, while at the same time keeping costs to a minimum, some services and facilities are shared by all the users on the network. Most commonly provided in this way are printers, data-processing systems, databases and high-capacity disk stores. The network itself is a shared resource. Not only the hardware but also the software used in the electronic office should be shared. For example, the electronic mail system, archiving programs, word-processing system, etc. are all suitable for sharing.
Access to external facilities Many office workers need to be able to access specialist information services, databases, libraries, data-transmission networks, and other computer-based services provided outside their own organisation, in addition to the public telephone network.
Communications facilities In order to link the office worker's personal workstation to other workstations and services, a communications network must be provided. This can take the form of a network based on the idea of the private telephone system, possibly even using the central telephone

exchange as the means for making connections between devices, or it can be a local area network of the type being considered in this book.

As mentioned earlier most effort so far has been spent on the provision of word-processing facilities in the office. This is because it is easy to see its advantages compared with traditional methods of text preparation and modification. Word processors can be stand-alone devices, but more advantages can be obtained by linking them together, and by sharing the use of a high-speed central disk store. In this way, a document can be typed by one person and become accessible electronically to several others for reading or for updating.

Some of the other services that can be provided by the electronic office are

Telex and Teletex   Two forms of international electronic mail services.

Facsimile   Electronic transmission of static pictures, hand-written text, etc. The distinguishing feature of facsimile images are that they cannot easily be placed into a coded form, so the image has to be scanned bit by bit and each element transmitted separately for assembling again at the destination.

Information   Corporate information databases or files of reference data particular to the job being performed. Personal information (diaries, planning, reports, etc.) also needs to be catered for.

Electronic mail   Mainly on site or within a single organisation, although the technique can be extended to external mail in limited quantities.

Data processing   Workstations provide only a limited amount of computing power, and this is often directed explicitly to supporting the office functions. Some workers need to access larger data-processing services, and this can be done through their workstation performing like a computer terminal.

Electronic conferencing   Conferencing facilities can be provided by extending the electronic mail service of the electronic office. It is particularly useful in situations where the people involved are out of the office frequently and it is difficult to organise a meeting to suit everyone.

Local area networks are essential ingredients in the electronic office since the individual workstations must be connected to each other and to shared resources for the system to work effectively. Because such large numbers of devices are involved in the average office, a traditional network of central processors linked to terminal/workstations by exclusive circuits would be difficult and expensive to install.

Although the local area network is going to be part of practically every electronic office system it must be invisible to the end-users. The average office worker will not want to be involved with setting up circuits to other workstations or processors whenever he is using a network service.

8.3 OTHER APPLICATIONS

Local area networks represent one of the many kinds of communication infrastructures that can be used to link computing equipment. A major difference between a local area network and other networks is the range of services that can be tailor-made for the particular group of users on that network. Because the network is confined to a small area, or a restricted group of users, special services can be provided, either as part of the network or available through it.

In addition to ordinary computer networking and electronic office functions, a local area network can be used to support new application areas, some of which are considered in the rest of this section.

Education   Teaching computing is made much easier if each student is given hands-on experience while under the supervision of the instructor. Microcomputers are ideal for teaching the basics of programming and file handling since each device is relatively cheap, making it feasible to provide one for each student to use. Linking them together during a class is also advantageous because then a separate high-capacity disk storage device can be shared, rather than each microcomputer having its own set of floppy-disk drives or other form of storage medium. A local area network is the obvious choice for linking microcomputers. The disk-storage device, or file-server as it is often called, can be configured to provide extra services to the users of the network. It can, for example, allow the supervisor to examine the files of each of the students, and even makes it possible for the screen display of one device to be seen by others in the network. Thus the supervisor can examine the conditions on one of the student's devices using his own workstation. The instructor can also demonstrate a technique at his workstation with the students seeing an exact copy of what he is doing on their own workstations. At the end of the class the workstations can be unplugged from the network and taken to another classroom.

Entertainment   The entertainment industry has been very quick to see the potential in integrated electronics and in microprocessor-controlled games. Local area networks could be employed to link these games, to provide two users with separate screens and controls for example, or to share storage facilities to enhance the facilities available.

Broadband local area networks have employed the equipment developed for the cable television market, so it is reasonable to suppose that broadband local area networking techniques for sharing channels may be adapted to provide access to centrally stored entertainment facilities, such as newspapers and games, which can be displayed on ordinary television receivers, in much the same way as viewdata.

Local area networks all provide the physical transmission medium, the method of controlling its use, an interface to the medium, addressing and routeing facilities and a data link service. The last feature enables blocks of data (which are not necessarily the same as the packets transported by the network itself, but are the blocks related to the device or application software using the network) to be transported reliably between devices attached to the network. Other facilities, built on these, are needed to provide a user-orientated service of the type normally expected in an on-line terminal system or computer network. The main facility is a service that provides a user with a 'connection' to another user, terminal or application, independently of the physical location on the network. To the user this connection looks like a dedicated point-to-point link. For some attached devices the requirement will be for a service that can support several independent conversations from one device to others simultaneously — a computer to several terminals being a typical example. For other devices, such as a simple terminal, only one conversation at a time can be supported, so the service should ensure that messages and packets from other devices on the network do not interrupt conversations already taking place.

Not all applications will require this type of service. Others will require a 'datagram' service in which each attached device can send individually addressed packets to a number of other devices without having to go to the trouble of setting up 'connections' first. It is then the responsibility of the end device, or some intelligent interface, to handle the incoming packets and decide to which application program or individual terminal or conversation they relate.

Further levels of sophistication can be built on these services as the customer and applications dictate.

8.4 INTEGRATED SERVICES

The phrase 'integrated services' refers to the use of digital data, voice, facsimile, text and visual information within a system in such a way that one complements the other. Integrating different types of information is uncommon as yet, although the situation is slowly changing.

It has been usual to install one network on a site to handle voice telephone traffic and nothing else, although, except for the telephone exchange itself, the network is used for only a small proportion of the total time. Each telephone on the system may be used for only a few minutes each day but a dedicated cable between it and the exchange is still needed. Similarly, computer and terminal networks have been specially built to serve their own needs, although the cables used follow many of the same routes as the telephone cables.

The Hasler Company in Switzerland set up their experimental SILK local area network in an attempt to rationalise the situation with regard to telephone and computer traffic. Their system was designed explicitly to allow all the site telephones to share the same cables with each other and with data services. The telephone handsets themselves are intelligent and can accept and reject calls made by other telephones on the network without the need for a separate exchange. Each telephone digitises the speech and transmits it in packet form to the other user. The bandwidth required to transmit voice conversations is not great when compared with some computer applications, especially when silent passages are not transmitted. A telephone exchange is required to handle calls only to and from external networks, such as the public telephone system.

The requirements of voice traffic differ from those of computer-generated information. In particular, computers demand that the stream of information is exactly correct, and if any error is detected the appropriate portion has to be retransmitted. It does not matter too much to a computer or a terminal if there are gaps of a few seconds between adjacent packets, but this would be extremely disturbing to the average telephone user. However, a person on the telephone can still understand a severely distorted signal and can fill in small portions of a conversation that are missed. At worst he can ask the other person to repeat them. Thus a network and its protocols which is built to support voice traffic is not concerned so much with absolute accuracy but more with rapid delivery.

This discussion of sharing voice and digital data on the same network serves to highlight some of the important points of integrated data-transmission systems. Each of the other forms of information that can, with advantage, share the same local area network has its own particular set of requirements. Facsimile, for example, can use quite slow circuits and each portion of the picture being transmitted can take a long time to be built up, but it must be accurate. Text processing demands a quick response on the workstation and the ability to move quickly from one file to another, or from one line to another within each file. Visual information can demand a range of requirements, from very high speed with no delays for real-time television, to low-speed systems where images are being built up slowly on graphic display terminals. Any local area network system used for integrated services must be capable of handling all the different forms of information that will be presented to it, and preferably should be able to tailor its services to the different requirements.

In addition to the integration of different forms of information within a local area network the system may need to integrate different networks: local and wide area, public and private data networks. Information that passes from one network to another changes from being subject to one set of procedures to being subject to another set. The networks may employ different capacity-sharing techniques or different transmission speeds. Thus a gateway device must exist which is physically attached to both networks and which can operate under both regimes.

The design of gateways is a complex subject, especially where the characteristics of the networks being linked differ considerably. Local area networks will often be linked to other networks providing a very much lower data-transmission rate. Thus, apart from having to provide the usual gateway functions of protocol and access method conversion, the gateway must be able to operate at two or more different speeds and must incorporate sufficient buffer space and suitable flow-control procedures to prevent the high-speed network from swamping it with information.

Project UNIVERSE [3] is an experimental project concerned with linking local area networks located in universities and other establishments in the UK through a satellite system. Local area networks are typified by high data-transmission rates with minimal delays between two points. Satellite networks, however, involve long delays in transmission although the actual transmission rate can be high. Project UNIVERSE will examine the problems of linking the two types of network and the functions of the gateways required.

8.5 TECHNOLOGICAL ADVANCES

Finally, we will survey some of the advances being made in technologies and techniques relevant to local area networks. Local area networks are partly the result of the revolution in cheap integrated electronic components making sophisticated data-communications equipment possible at a reasonable price. It would be naive to suppose that the complexity and cheapness of the electronics has reached its peak, so there is every likelihood that local area networks will continue to develop along the lines already indicated by the current systems, but incorporate a wider range of facilities and use higher transmission speeds.

The access methods now used for local area networks fall into three main categories: those based on carrier sense multiple access (CSMA) baseband bus methods; the empty slot ring technique; and the register insertion ring technique. Broadband networks generally use a combination of the well-established, frequency-division multiplexing way of dividing a wide frequency channel into a number of narrower channels, together with a CSMA method for sharing these narrow channels. All these techniques have one feature in common: they are relatively easy to implement using standard electronic components and the resulting interface devices are not excessively expensive.

Token passing is a technique that is easy to implement on a true ring, since it employs a very similar method of access to the well-established, register insertion technique. A few manufacturers of computer systems have used token-passing rings for their local communications. For bus networks, however, the token-passing idea, although possible in principle, is difficult to implement successfully in practice. Briefly, the problems arise from the fact that a device may or may not be switched on when attached to a bus so there is no guarantee that that device has heard and received the token passed to it. If it is not listening then it will no pass the token on to the next device, so some procedure must be devised to create one, and only one, token if the original one is lost. If a device is not being passed the token (because it has previously been switched off, for example) then some way for it to request to be sent the token must be agreed. The result is a complex procedure that requires a significant amount of intelligence in the interface devices for it to operate properly. The technique, however, holds out much promise, because a well-designed token-passing bus could be extremely efficient in allowing every user wanting to use the network to obtain a fair share of the capacity but without time being wasted on devices not transmitting. A token-passing bus can be specifically designed to give priority to some devices if their transmission requirements warrant it. No other system for baseband buses appears to have the same advantages. To become a viable alternative however, suitably cheap interfaces are required which may demand purpose-built chips to handle the access protocol similar to those for Ethernet.

Broadband systems are also ideal candidates for enhancement because of the quantity of bandwidth available that is still largely unused. Quantity production of the special modems required will significantly reduce their price.

Optical fibres offer the potential for much wider bandwidths, better transmission characteristics and longer lengths than ordinary metal cables. The major problems with using an optical fibre system for a local area network are the high cost and the difficulty of making connections to it. The cost of the cable is certain to reduce as more of it is used for trunk cables and the techniques for making it improve. Various ways of tapping into the cables are being devised and this should result in simpler connections in the near future.

Another factor that will have a very significant impact on local area networks is the development of advanced local telephone exchanges, in particular the digital PABX (Private Automatic Branch Exchange). The digital PABX need not be confined to interconnecting telephones but can be used to handle digital signals from computing devices and can even act as a gateway between separate local and wide area networks. Techniques have been devised to allow a piece of digital equipment to share a line with a telephone, enabling each to remain independent and able to be connected to different destinations simultaneously.

In summary, although 10 Mbps bus and ring systems are currently the most common local area networks, we can expect to see 50 or 100 Mbps networks using rings, baseband buses or star-shaped systems (using a PABX at the hub) in the next few years. Broadband networks are likely to increase in sophistication as physical media and devices with a greater bandwidth are introduced.

8.6 CONCLUSIONS

Interest in local area networks has grown very rapidly, partly because users see them as a cheap method of interconnecting large numbers of relatively inexpensive devices, and partly because they appear to solve some of the problems of incompatibility between items of equipment. Certainly a cheap local area network can be provided to allow individual devices to send streams of information from one device to another. If, however, the devices involved use different character sets and high-level protocols, the local area network itself will seldom solve the incompatibility problem. Networks that can handle different protocols and character sets, and that provide the conversion facilities required, are much more complex and expensive than basic local area networks.

The next generation of local networks will consist of an underlying communications system with sophisticated interfaces built on it suitable for handling a very wide variety of possible devices. Some networks will be complete systems, an electronic office system for example, in which the devices supplied are designed to work with each other and which use a particular type of network. The actual local area network in such systems is just a component, albeit an essential one, of the complete system.

Most of the devices that will use a local area network will contain intelligence to a greater or lesser degree, and non-intelligent terminals will become rare, since they need an intelligent interface in order to use a local area network. Since the interconnected devices will be intelligent and capable of processing applications software, the networks will in effect be fully interconnected distributed processing systems, with resource sharing a feature of most of them.

The most interesting aspects of local area networks are the possibilities that they give for integrating data, voice, text and other forms of information on the same network. The scope for saving on cabling costs within a site is very considerable. This is rather a long-term goal since current systems tend to be aimed mainly at the data-transmission market, sometimes with the inclusion of voice. Broadband systems are certainly capable of handling all forms of information transmission and it seems likely that these will undergo the most rapid development in integrated communications services. Equipment that can take advantage of the facilities offered by mixing digital data with other forms of information is available already in limited quantities.

REFERENCES

1 Price, S. G., *Introducing the Electronic Office*, NCC Publications, Manchester, 1979.
2 Welch, W. J. and Wilson, P. A., *Electronic Mail Systems — A Practical Evaluation Guide*, NCC Publications, Manchester, 1981.
3 Kirstein, P. T., Daniels, R., Burren, J., Griffiths, J. W. R., King, D., Needham, R. and McDowell, C., 'The UNIVERSE project', *Proceedings of the 6th International Conference on Computer Communications, London*, September 1982.

Glossary

ANALOGUE TRANSMISSION Transmission of a continuously varying signal.

APPLICATION A user-related task which can be performed using a computer system.

APPLICATION PROGRAM OR SOFTWARE A set of computer instructions directly associated with an application executed by the computer.

ARCHITECTURE A framework for a computer or communications system which defines its functions, interfaces and procedures.

BANDWIDTH The difference between the upper and lower frequencies that are available for transmission.

BASEBAND Information is encoded directly on to the transmission medium. Only one signal is present on the medium at any time.

BROADBAND A method of using a transmission medium having a wide frequency bandwidth. Several signals can be carried simultaneously by allocating different channels to separate frequency bands.

BROADCAST All devices on the system (network or medium) are capable of receiving all signals transmitted by others.

CATV (Community Antenna Television) The distribution of television broadcasts by means of cables from a central receiver.

CCITT (Comité Consultatif International Télégraphique et Téléphonique) The international body through which the national telecommunications bodies coordinate their activities.

CHANNEL A means of transporting information signals. Several channels can share the same physical circuit.

CIRCUIT SWITCHING A method of connecting together two users of a transmission service which allocates a circuit for their exclusive use for the duration of the call.

COLLISION When two information signals attempt to use the same channel simultaneously and their information content is corrupted.

CONCENTRATION The function of channelling information from a number of users on to a smaller number of higher-capacity links. A *concentrator* is the device that performs this function.

CONTENTION   When more than one user attempts to use the same channel simultaneously.

CSMA (Carrier Sense Multiple Access)   A method of sharing a channel. Before transmitting any information the sender looks for the presence of a carrier signal, indicating that the channel is already being used. If no signal is present the sender can transmit.

DATAGRAM   A single packet that is routed without reference by the network to any other datagram being sent.

DISTRIBUTED DATABASE   An organised collection of data that has been subdivided or copied, and distributed among several different locations in a distributed computing system.

DISTRIBUTED PROCESSING   The distribution of information processing among several different locations.

DISTRIBUTED SYSTEM   An information-processing system in which a number of individual processors at different locations are linked together so that they can cooperate.

END-USER   A person who uses an information-processing system.

FILE   An organised collection of data records that can be accessed by name.

GATEWAY   A computer system or exchange in one network that allows access to and from another network.

HDLC (High-level Data Link Control)   A protocol designed for data transmission which is data independent.

HOST   A computer system on which applications can be executed and which also provides a service to users of a computer network.

INFORMATION PROCESSOR   A computer that provides computing, data storage and data-manipulation services.

INTERFACE   A boundary between two devices or two pieces of software across which the form and functions of the signals that pass it are specified.

ISO (International Organization for Standardization)   The body that exists to promote the development of standards in the world. Membership consists of national organisations that are most representative of standardisation in their countries.

LAYER   A set of logically related functions that are grouped together.

LOGICAL CONNECTION   A connection in which the means of information transfer may not exist as a real physical entity for the duration of the call.

MANCHESTER ENCODING   A technique for sending digital information serially, in which the data and clock signals are combined.

MESSAGE   A logically related collection of data to be moved.

MODEM   A piece of equipment that converts digital signals into analogue signals for transmission. The modem also performs the reverse function.

MULTIPLEXING   The use of a single physical link for two or more simultaneous separate transmissions. A multiplexer is the device that performs this function.

MULTIPOINT or MULTIDROP CONNECTION   A circuit that is connected to several different destinations.

NODE   A point at which two or more communication circuits meet. Commonly used in computer networks to describe a point where processing is performed.

OPEN SYSTEMS INTERCONNECTION   Standardised procedures for the exchange of information between terminals, computers, people, networks, etc.

PACKET   A block of data with a defined format containing control and data fields.

PACKET SWITCHING   A term used in a data-transmission network that is designed to carry the data in the form of packets. The data, in packets, is passed to the network, which uses the control information contained in each packet to transmit the packet to the correct destination.

PHYSICAL CONNECTION   A transmission circuit between two or more users which usually consists of electrical conductors along which signals are transmitted.

POLLING   A process whereby terminals are invited one at a time to transmit information.

PROTOCOL   A set of rules to ensure a meaningful communication between cooperating partners.

REAL TIME   Normally used to describe the situation where a computer is used to control and monitor directly a manufacturing process.

REPEATER   A device used to regenerate, amplify and retransmit signals.

RESOURCE   A hardware or software component of a system that can serve a user requirement (for example, printer, computer system file).

SESSION   When two software processes, users, resources, or other components in a network, are connected together for the purpose of exchanging information, they are said to be in session.

STATION   A single addressable unit on a network.

SWITCHING   In computer or communication networks, switching is the process by which services or data are directly made available to the appropriate user.

SYSTEM   A collection of computers, associated software, peripherals, terminals, human users, etc., that form an autonomous whole, capable of information processing.

TERMINAL   A device that allows an end-user to input data to and receive data from an information-processing system.

TRANSCEIVER   A transmitter/receiver through which devices can access the network.

TRANSPARENT   A communications link is said to be transparent when it does not alter in any way the contents of the messages it transmits.

VIRTUAL CIRCUIT   A call using a virtual circuit employs real physical connections which the transmission service may use for other calls made by other subscribers.

Index*

*Major entries are enumerated in *italic* type.